GW01607229

NOTES ON THE OLDER CHURCHES IN THE FOUR WELSH DIOCESES

By
Sir Stephen Richard Glynne, Bart.

A facsimile reprint of a series of articles that were published posthumously between 1884 and 1902

in two volumes of which this is

Vol. II.

ISBN 1861 431 252

LLANERCH PRESS. Cribyn, 2004.

The Late Sir STEPHEN R. GLYNNE, Bart.

RADNORSHIRE:—ELWEL DEANERY.

Disserth (St. Cewydd).

This church has nave and chancel without aisles, and western tower. The latter is rude, and without buttresses or stringcourses, but with embattled parapet and two tiers of windows; those of the belfry of two lights have rather a Decorated look. The west window is square-headed, of two lights. The tower arch is intercepted by a gallery. The east window is Perpendicular, of four lights, and has wood mullions. Just under it externally is a flat arched recess. The other windows are mostly modern, of the worst kind, except one square-headed and labelled, of three lights, trifoliated—a late Perpendicular on the south of the chancel. There is no chancel arch; the chancel has a coved roof with ribs, and the nave is ceiled.

Gladestry (St. Mary).

October 28, 1870.

A nice church, fairly restored, comprising nave with north aisle, western tower with shingled spire, chancel, and south porch. The nave is divided from the aisle by three pointed arches on octagonal pillars with capitals. There are some square-headed windows in the nave of three lights, of rather Edwardian character. Near the east of the nave, on the south, is a very long lancet, and a smaller one near the tower. The chancel-arch is pointed, rising at once from the wall. The east window is a fine Perpendicular of four lights; on the south is a plain trefoil piscina, a priest's door, and a three-light Perpendicular window. The interior is fitted with open seats. The tower is massive and plain, opening into the nave by a pointed doorway only. It has no buttress, but one stringcourse; three single-light openings and more ornamental belfry windows of Perpendicular character, one single with ogee arch and panelling, one of two cinquefoiled lights square-headed.

The spire is shingled ; the steeple generally resembling that of Kington. The nave has a ridge-crest and bell-gable at its east end. In the churchyard is the shaft of a cross raised on high steps.

Glascwm (St. David).

October, 1870.

This church is in a pretty, retired site, and consists of nave and chancel, with a south porch and no tower or bell-cot. There is a chancel-arch, pointed with plain soffit. There are some good Perpendicular windows of three lights, especially on the south side of the nave. There is a priest's door on the south of the chancel. The east window is closed. Over the east end of the nave is some ornamental panelling, marking the rood-loft place. The chancel has a coved roof, with ribs and bosses. In the roof of the nave is some trefoil wood-work. The porch is very large, and has square-headed windows trefoiled. The churchyard is very large and steep, commanding a pretty rural view.

Aberedw (St. Cewydd).

September 8, 1851.

This church is in a lovely situation, on a rock overhanging the river Edw near its confluence with the Wye. It is entirely Third Pointed of rather late date, and consists of a chancel and nave with west tower and large north porch. The work is rather coarse. The porch is highly picturesque, and is entirely of wood, with feathered gable and pierced trefoils in the framework above the outer door. Within it is a stone bench on each side. The tower is rude, with a stringcourse but no buttress, two other slits for belfry windows on the east and west, and one on the north and south. It is covered with a pointed roof, and opens into the nave only by a door. The chancel is lower than the nave, and not ill-developed, but there is no chancel arch. The chancel roof is coved. with panelling, having ribs and bosses. The rood-screen remains of plain Third Pointed work. The east window is closed up, and no trace of it perceptible. The other windows are mostly square-headed. The altar is raised on three high steps, and in the east wall is a square recess. The font has a circular bowl, on an octagonal stem. The nave is ceiled. The interior is neat and clean, but part of the west end used for a school. The accustomed entrance is on the north. The north porch is modern. The new prayer-desk faces west. The adjacent rock, wood, and river scenery is enchanting.

Boughrood.

May 20, 1851.

A small church, in a lovely situation near to the Wye. It consists of nave and chancel without aisles, and a small western steeple, of stone in its lower part, having slits for openings and a wooden belfry. A south porch is of mixed stone and wood. The chancel arch is a very rude, pointed one. In the nave are some bad modern windows, and two single ones with trefoiled heads; of the latter kind is also one in the chancel. The east window is a modern imitation of Middle Pointed with a transom, containing indifferent painted glass. There is a handsome new font, the bowl octagonal, with Middle Pointed panelling and octagonal stem. The old font, with plain circular bowl, is in the churchyard. The interior is pewed, but tolerably neat. The churchyard is of very large size, and only partially used.

Clyro (St. Michael).

December 28, 1870.

This church has been wholly rebuilt, save the tower, which appears old, and is low and strongly built, having a saddle roof with gables east and west, and some plain single openings, some round-headed, some mere slits. The nave has north aisle, divided by an arcade of four pointed arches, and the whole of the chancel and nave are in creditable Edwardian character.

Llanano.

May 10, 1851.

A very small church, in a lonely situation near the Ithon, with nave and chancel having no exterior distinction, a south porch, and wooden belfry at the west end. The windows are mostly wretched, but there is one obtuse lancet on the north side of the chancel which may be early. The porch is of wood, rude but picturesque. The great feature of this little church is its fine rood-loft, which is in a very perfect state. It is of the panelled kind, with niches, and the usual vine-leaf cornice. Each compartment below has tracery, and the west front is much richer than the eastern. The font has a circular bowl on an octagon. The west end of the nave is partitioned off for a school.

Llanbadarn Vynydd (St. Paternus).

This church has only one space for nave and chancel, with a large south porch and a modern bell set over the west end. The roof is open, with collars and quatrefoiled timbers, which are curiously seen externally in the east gable intermixed with plaster. The east window is a mutilated Decorated one of three lights—one on the south, of two lights, is of the same kind and in fair condition. The other windows modern and bad. There is a large buttress at the west end. The interior is dreary. Part of the rood-screen remains.

Bleddfa (St. Mary).

This church has merely a nave and chancel undivided, with a south porch, and a wooden belfry at the west end. The chancel is nearly equal in length to the nave, a difference being perceptible in the roof. Another remarkable feature is that the ground abruptly rises at the west end (not gradually, as at Pilleth), so as to mount up that part very high. The exterior walls are whitewashed. There are some single lancets both in the nave and chancel which are original, but several windows are modern and very poor, especially that at the east end. There is a pointed recess in the north wall by the sacrarium. The interior is dreary, but in less bad state than most of the Radnorshire churches. The porch is rude. The cemetery very large, but no graves on the north.

Heyop (St. David).

This church has the usual undivided nave and chancel, with south porch and a low, rude tower at the west end, which has the local pointed roof covered with tiles. The tower has no buttresses, and its openings are mere slits. The exterior whitewashed. Internally, the pulpit is mean ; there are a few old open benches, and the altar is encroached upon by pews. The ceiling flat and modern ; most of the windows wretched and mutilated. One on the south of the chancel is Perpendicular, square-headed, of two lights ; two others in the nave are square-headed, of three or four lights, apparently Elizabethan, having moulded woodwork. On the south is a rude slit, now closed. The chancel is divided by a fair wood screen of Perpendicular character. On the south of the altar is an oblong recess. The font has a plain octagonal bowl on a stem. The north wall of the chancel extends wider than that of the nave. The porch is flagged, but mostly of wood.

Llanbister.

May 9, 1851.

A church of very singular appearance, though by no means from its beauty. It consists of one space, of which the eastern part forms the chancel, and is distinguished by being raised up several steps, in consequence of the great rise in the uneven ground, and also separated by a plain and mutilated screen. But the most curious feature is the position of the steeple at the east end of the chancel, exactly behind the altar. There is, therefore, neither east nor west window, though there is no particular reason for the absence of the latter. The west end of the nave is, according to South Wales fashion, partitioned off for a school. The whole has a neglected look within, yet rather striking, the space being wide and with a rude, open roof. The ground in the churchyard is most curiously uneven, and its sudden fall from the west end seems to prevent the erection of a steeple there. There is also a very sudden rise on the north, on which side are no windows, except one of rather Romanesque look, which is closed. There is a square-headed one of five lights on the south side of the chancel, with a window-seat. The tower is low and large, with scarce any architectural character, but having a tiled roof and a pointed wooden belfry. It opens into the east wall of the church by a plain door. There is a south porch near the west end of the nave, and in it a benatura or stoup. The font is octagonal, small and poor.

Pilleth (St. Mary).

A small church in a remarkable situation, quite lonely, high up on an eminence. The ground is very steep, and descends rapidly from the east end, so that here occurs the unusual feature of a church descending from the west towards the east. There is no separate chancel or aisle, but a south porch and odd-looking, short, squat western tower—the walls wholly white-washed. The porch is of wood, and somewhat picturesque. The roof is open, with panelling and arched ribs. The chancel is divided from the nave by a fairly-preserved wood screen, having plain panelling. The east window is modern, but one at the south-east is fair Decorated, with ogee head, of two lights, without hood or continuing arch, and there is one similar at the north-east. The tower has on the west a plain Perpendicular window, with central longitudinal division, and a large square projection to the south-west, with slits to light a staircase. The tower is covered by a heavy, saddle-shaped roof. Its figure is most curious, perched up on the hill-side, but the situation is picturesque and interesting.

WHITTON (ST. DAVID).

A mean church, small, dark, and neglected, consisting of a single body, with low western tower. The east window is square-headed, of two lights, and fair Edwardian; all other windows modern and mutilated. There is a post-Reformation screen, inscribed, dividing the chancel; a mean porch is on the south near the tower, and a doorway on the north of the chancel close to the east end, apparently modern. The chancel is ceiled and whitewashed. The font has a small octagonal bowl on stem. A rude arched doorway opens from the nave to the tower. The tower is singularly rude, and constructed partly of wood and partly of stone, without regular architectural order, but reaching very little above the roof of the nave, and having the somewhat characteristic pointed roof of tiles common in Radnorshire. The cemetery is remarkably large, the site beautiful.

NOTES ON THE OLDER CHURCHES

IN THE

FOUR WELSH DIOCESES.

BY THE LATE SIR STEPHEN R. GLYNNE, BART.

(*Continued from p. 57.*)

ILSTON (ST. ILTYD).

August, 1851.

AN interesting specimen of a church of Gower, lately put into a state of order and repair, and beautifully situated on a sloping bank finely shaded by trees. It comprises a chancel with south chapel, nave, and a tower on the south side of the nave. The latter is peculiar, being low and rude, and unusually large and massive, partaking quite of a castellated character. It has no openings, but mere slits and no stringcourse, a plain battlement, which in the centre of the south side rises into a low gable, and a roof of saddle form. The east and west faces have corbel tables under the battlement. The tower is vaulted, and opens to the nave by a low, rude, obtuse arch. The chancel arch is pointed, and springs immediately from the wall without moulding. The west-end of the nave has a middle-pointed window of two lights. On the north is a lancet trefoiled, and one transitional from first to middle-pointed; also of two lights with foiled circle above and no hood. There seem to have been no windows originally on the north. The east window has three lancet lights beneath a pointed arch, the hood having crowned heads for corbels. On the north of the chancel is a lancet restored, if not quite new. The ground being very uneven causes an unusual ascent eastward, and there are two sets of steps in the chancel. The chancel arch is not in the centre, whence arises a crooked appearance. The font has an octagonal bowl on a similar base. In the north wall of the chancel is an arched recess. The chapel on the south of the chancel is perhaps debased, with little architectural character. The roofs are newly slated, and there is a good cross on the east gable and on the west. There is a rude arch between the chancel and the south chapel. The whole interior is very neat, with new open benches, and the general appearance of this church contrasts agreeably with the neglected state of most churches in Gower.

The churchyard is beautiful and secluded.

LLANGYVELACH (ST. CYVELACH).

June 4th, 1860.

This church has a nave and chancel, with chapel to the north of the latter, and a detached tower on the south of the churchyard. The nave has been rebuilt in very poor Gothic. The chancel, which is of unusual length, perhaps retains the original walls. The chancel arch is obtuse, of doubtful character; on the north is a flat arched doorway; and opening to the north chapel from the church is a rude flat arch. This chapel is full of marble monuments; south of the chancel appear some ruined walls, probably of vestry or chapel. The tower is quite distinct from the church, on an elevated spot in the burying-ground. It is rude and characteristic of the country, with little of architectural feature. The parapet has a low gable in the centre on the east and west, and is embattled on the other sides. There is neither string nor buttress. A pointed doorway on the west, belfry windows square-headed and divided by a mullion, and some small slit-like openings.

The churchyard is very spacious and the ground uneven, but there are very few graves on the north side.

Oystermouth (All Saints).

1836.

The church has a west tower, nave and chancel, with much of the singular and rude character of the neighbouring churches. The tower is of great strength, and has a large battlement with billet cornice under it. There are no buttresses, but a large projecting stair turret on the south side up the whole height of the tower. The tower is divided into two stages, the apertures all small and narrow, with square heads. In the belfry story there are three, of unequal size. Within the north porch is a pointed door, having arch mouldings and dripstone with head-corbels. The windows are chiefly Perpendicular, square-headed, of three lights, with labels; one on the north of the chancel, of two lights, of rather superior style. On the south of the nave is a trefoil lancet. The chancel arch is low, pointed, but with scarcely any curve, and resting upon imposts. On the south side of it is a projection opening by a pointed arch, and containing a staircase which must have led to the rood-loft. In this projecting turret is a small lancet window. There are many bad modern windows, and the chancel has been much altered. It has an excrescence both on the north and south sides—one used as a vestry—but they do not seem to be modern, the northern one having a tolerable Perpendicular window. The east window had once three lancets, one only of which is now open. The font is placed in the chancel, and is a square bowl scalloped at its base, upon a cylindrical shaft with square base. The interior is very plain and bare. The graves in the churchyard are planted with various flowers in the form of the coffin, marked out in pebbles. From the churchyard is an enchanting view over Swansea Bay, the Mumbles, and the fine ruins of the neighbouring castle. The tower is oblong.

The castle must have been very grand when perfect,

and a very considerable portion yet remains, though dismantled, and more traces of architectural features than are often met with in castellated remains. The situation is majestic and elevated.

Pennard (St. Mary).

August, 1851.

This church is more modernised than most others in Gower. It has only a chancel, nave, and small north transept, with a small steeple at the west end, crowned by a modern spire. The said turret is oblong, the longest sides being east and west, and has a battlement with corbel table and a slit-like opening in the belfry story. There is also a second corbel table lower down; no buttresses; on the west side a double window of two ogee-headed trefoiled lights, now closed. There are no windows in the north of the chancel, and those on the south of the nave are modernised. The chancel arch is an obtusely pointed one, on imposts, and very plain. The chancel has on the south a low lancet window closed, and another lancet with a hood-moulding of bold toothed ornament. The east window is Third Pointed, square-headed, of two lights, labelled. Over the east gable is a large cross. The roofs are modern and slated, and the whole is in a neat state.

Cheriton, Co. Glam. (St. Catwg).

August 28, 1861.

An interesting church, and differing in some measure from the Gower type. It consists of a nave and chancel, with a tower in the centre between them, and a porch south of the nave. The porch is, according to the custom of the neighbourhood, very large, and has stone seats. Within it is an Early English doorway, remarkable for its ornate character so rare in south Wales, and resembling those of Llanaber and Llanbadarn. It has two courses of mouldings and a hood, with banded shafts having caps of foliage. On the south side of the nave is one lancet window and one bad modern one.

The west window is a new Decorated one of two lights. There is a rood door high up in the north of the nave near the tower arch. The nave has recently been fitted with open benches of plain character, and some improvements have been effected in the condition of the church. The tower opens to the nave and chancel by pointed arches, not at all similar: the eastern has two orders rising from pretty corbel shafts on corbel heads, having octagonal caps and neck mouldings, the outer merely chamfered, but on impost moulding, which is carried along the whole. The eastern arch chamfered on corbel shaft, with octagonal capitals and neck mouldings; the western on ditto, but with foliage and no neck moulding on the north (which has also a foliaged corbel); on the south on octagonal moulded impost, with neither neck moulding nor foliage. The western arch is of rather richer character, and springs from corbel shafts, of which the northern has a foliaged cap without neck moulding, and is set on a corbel of foliage. That on the south has merely an octagonal moulded impost, without neck moulding or foliage. All these are fluted, and good Early English. The chancel is very small, so that the space under the tower should form the Chorus Cantorum. There is a rude open staircase against the north wall of the tower seen from within. There are some indistinct openings at the north-west of the chancel. On the north of the chancel is a closed lancet, and a flat arched recess elbowed. On the S. are two lancets restored, and traces of a piscina. The east window has two trefoil-headed lights, common in South Wales. The old font has a circular bowl broken; that in use is octagonal on stem.

The tower is rude, has coarse battlements and corbel table, and lighted only by slit-like apertures. It has a small saddle-back within the parapet, and running east and west. The rood-loft was west of the tower. There is a very considerable ascent towards the east, owing to the unevenness of the ground.

Llanmadoc (St. Madoc).

September 24, 1848.

A small church, with a chancel, nave, west tower, and south porch, of the usual rude and coarse sort. The tower is low, with saddle-back roof gabled at the east and west sides, and having a corbel table on the north and south. On the west side in the gable is a plain slit, and there is no other opening in it whatever. It presents a solid wall to the nave, with only a small door in it. There are no north windows of any kind; the roof is new, and the southern windows of the nave modernised. The chancel arch, as in the other Gower churches, is very low, of round shape upon imposts, with a large space of solid wall above it. On the north, at some height, is the rood door. There is a very old square font set low on the south side of the chancel arch. On the south-west of the chancel is a closed lychnoscope; the other chancel windows (both on the east and south side) are single trefoil-headed lancets, having internally a double arch over them. Under the east window is a rude square projection, which has some appearance of a rough reredos. In the east wall is also a bracket.

Llanddewi in Gower (St. David).

August 2, 1871.

A small neglected church, much out of repair; consists of nave, chancel, south porch and west tower. The tower is low, of very rude construction, and little architectural character; without buttresses, but having the north and south sides gabled at the top. There is a battlement and corbel table on the east side; the openings are mere slits, save the north belfry window, which is

Pointed. The chancel arch is very rude, and of obtuse form; but one half has mouldings, the other not. On the north side of it is an obtusely-pointed recess. There is a trace of a similar arched recess on the south of the chancel arch. On the north of the nave is a Norman window, much splayed, but closed. On the south is a single-light window with ogee head. In the chancel on the north is a trefoil-headed lancet; at the north-east, a two-light window without foliation.

Other windows are modern. The porch is large with stone seats, the doorway Pointed.

Llangenith (St. Cenith).

September 24, 1848.

The largest church in Gower; but, like all the others, without aisles. The nave, however, is capacious, and there is a fairly-developed chancel. The tower stands on the north side of the nave in place of a transept, and there is a large north porch containing stone seats. The chancel arch is a plain Pointed one upon imposts; there is a rood door on the south side, and a stone bench along both sides of the chancel. Near the south-east angle of the chancel is an indication of rude steps against the wall. On the south side of the altar is a square recess. The east window is modern Pointed of three lights; on the south of the chancel are two windows of two lights, surmounted by a flat arched opening to the interior; another has trefoil-headed lights. In the nave, on the south side, is a small square-headed window set obliquely, which has the appearance of a hagioscope. The nave has some Welsh-looking windows of two lights on the south, but none on the north. The tower opens to the nave by a small doorway in the wall, and is very strongly built and not square: being larger from east to west than from north to south. It has no buttresses, and only a few small slits for openings. There is a battlement on the east and west sides, and a saddle-back roof. Under the battlement a corbel table. The font has a square bowl scalloped below upon a cylindrical stem. In the south wall of the nave, under a window, is the effigy of a knight, much mutilated; and in the chancel two slabs with sculptured crosses. The roof of the chancel is in very bad order, and there is no pavement, but the bare earth in great part of the church.

The outer walls have been partly whitewashed.

Nicholaston (St. Nicholas).

July, 1836.

An extremely small church, with only a diminutive low nave and chancel, and a bell-gable over the west end. The situation quite solitary, on a height overlooking Oxwich Bay. There is a large south porch. The west window, a single lancet now closed; the eastern, a double lancet. On the north another lancet stopped, and on the south a poor square-headed Perpendicular window. The chancel arch rude and pointed, upon imposts; the font a square bowl on a cylindrical shaft.

Oxwich.

September 25, 1848.

A small church with chancel and nave only, and a western tower; very beautifully situated on a woody, high bank looking over the lovely bay. The tower has, as usual, rather a castellated character, and in its lowest part forms a porch. In the porch are stone benches; the west door rude and plain, and over it is a two-light window with three-foiled ogee lights. The battlement is rough and broken, and under it is a corbel table. The openings are very few and those only narrow slits; there are two strings of division, one near the base which, like others in this country, bulges out. There are no buttresses. The roofs are slated, the chancel is small, its east window modern Pointed of two lights. The east window is not in the centre.

In the north wall of the chancel is a fine ogee sepulchral arch, projecting outward very considerably. This arch has crockets, finial and double feathering with foliated spandrels. Beneath it are two effigies with hands joined in prayer; the recess is very deep. The chancel is small, its arch very low, mis-shapen and obtuse, with a great mass of solid wall about it. The roofs are plain and open. The windows are square-headed without foils; some appear modern. The churchyard is very picturesque, and the graves adorned with various flowers and evergreens, each grave being marked out by pebbles following the shape of the coffin. In the churchyard is a holy well in a rocky recess. The pews are neat, plain and new. It is probable that there were originally no windows on the north side, which is generally the case in South Wales.

Penrice (St. Andrew).

1836.

This church is on a very elevated situation, surrounded by fine trees, and adjoining the park. The churchyard presents a scene of great beauty, and the graves are adorned with thyme, heartsease, and box plants. The church has a west tower, nave, north transept, south porch, corresponding in size with the opposite transept and chancel. The tower is in the rude style prevalent in the southern part of South Wales, with a battlement and cornice of billets under it; no buttress or division, but four heights of plain loop-hole openings. The tower is hollow within, having no floors. The south porch has quite the appearance of a transept; it is entered from without by a plain pointed arch, and the door within is also plain and pointed. On its west side is a small trefoil lancet. The north transept has a window, apparently Decorated but much mutilated. There is an old window on the north side of two lights within an arch, surmounted by a square frame: this may be of late work. There is, in fact, very little architectural character about the church. The tower opens to the nave by a small pointed doorway. The chancel arch is semicircular, but ornamented in stucco in the style of the seventeenth century, in which style also the chancel has been altered, and an ugly east window inserted. There is an ascent of steps to the chancel, and along its side walls a low stone bench. On the south side is a low window, or lychnoscope, of Perpendicular character; also a two-light window with ogee heads trefoiled, also Perpendicular. The font is set in the west wall, an octagonal bowl on shaft of similar form with square base. There is much ivy on the south side of the church. The adjacent park presents glorious sylvan scenery, amidst which are the picturesque ruins of the ancient castle.

In Penrice churchyard is a gravestone of *dosd'âne* shape, with cross, to the late Sir Christopher Cole.

Port Eynon (St. Cadoc).

September 25, 1848.

This church has a chancel and nave, a modern north chapel and a south porch. Over the west end is a gable belfry, with two open arches for bells. The chancel arch is very low, rude, obtuse, and ill-shaped, springing from imposts with a considerable space of wall, on the north side of which is another low pointed arch, now blocked. The chancel has two windows, which have two trefoil-headed lights, opening to the interior by a wide pointed arch. There is no east window, and the altar is set at right angles with the east wall. There are two brackets also on the east wall, and on the south side an oblong recess. The windows of the church are all modern. The font is Norman, the bowl square upon a stem of clustered shafts set upon a square plinth. There is a benatura in the porch.

Reynaldstone (St. George).

August 22, 1849.

A small church in Gower; having only a chancel and nave, south porch and small bell-cot at the west end, with two bells. The chancel arch is a very rude Pointed one, and to the south of it is a hagioscope. There were no original north windows: a very usual circumstance in this locality. There is a rude projection on the north near the chancel arch, probably connected with the rood-loft. On the south of the chancel is an odd obtuse lancet, and a curious hagioscope.

Rhosilly.

September 24, 1848.

A long church consisting of chancel and nave, with small western tower and a south porch. The east window is modern Pointed, of two lights, the north and south windows of the chancel each a wide lancet, now closed. There is a trefoil-headed niche on the south side under a window, but there is no remaining trace of a piscina. There is also a lychnoscope on the south, now closed. The chancel arch is a very plain Pointed one. The roofs are open ; the floor is bare clay. The south door within the porch is Norman, but pointed with chevron mouldings and shafts. Within the porch, stone benches ; also a stone bench along the east end of the chancel. The windows are very few in the nave, and those very narrow and small. The steeple has the north and south sides gabled, and only a few slits for openings. It has an outer west door, and another opening into the nave. The font has a square bowl, scalloped on two sides, upon a short stem scarcely to be seen, and set on a square plinth. There is a glorious view from the churchyard over the sea, from the Worm's Head.

ARCHDEACONRY OF CARDIGAN—DEANERY OF ULTRA AERON.

LLANILAR (ST. HILARY).

The church has nave and chancel only, with a tower

Llanilar Church before Restoration.

at the west end. The tower is rather low but remarkably massive, without buttresses or stringcourses, swelling outward at the base. It has an embattled parapet, and carries a short spire. At the north-east is a square stair-turret; has some plain narrow openings, one at the west is arched. The south porch has a plain Pointed doorway; the north door is closed. The windows are nearly all poor modern Gothic, but the walls are old, and there is on the north of the sacrarium an original lancet, perfectly plain and open as a window. The original roof remains, of open timbers, with quatrefoil in the framework in Welsh fashion.

There is no chancel arch; the nave is paved, neat, but dreary; there is a priest's door.

Llanfihangel Geneu'r glyn, Co. Cardigan (St. Michael).

A cruciform church of the awkward Welsh fashion, without arches at the crossing, and having a wooden modern belfry rising from the centre. There are no aisles. The walls may possibly be original, but not one ancient feature is left evident. The windows are of the vilest, and there are none at all on the north side of the nave. The east window is perhaps Elizabethan: square, with central mullion. The roof has flat modern ceiling; the whole is pewed, and the interior very dreary. The font is a plain octagon. The ground rises very much to the west.

The churchyard is most remarkable for its quiet and picturesque beauty, and stretches to the west up a steep hill, thickly shaded with trees, amongst which appear the gravestones; there is a lych gate.

Llanfihangel in Creuddyn (S. Michael).

A cruciform church of some dignity, though rude in architecture, having a large central tower; there are no aisles. There is a south porch, and the church bears evidence of improvement, especially in the chancel. Altogether in far better case than the generality of Cardiganshire churches.

The interior walls have been stripped of whitewash, and the seats are chiefly open. The nave and transepts have ribbed roofs of a plain kind; the chancel is coved and panelled. The tower stands upon four very rude pointed arches, with strong piers having imposts. The east window has been renewed, is Perpendicular, but simply of three lights, without foils, within a pointed arch. On the north of the chancel is a trefoiled single-light window. On the south the windows are poor Perpendicular.

The windows of the transept are rude, square-headed, and poor; others are still worse. The chancel is neat, and the altar-cloth is a new one of red cloth. The font has an octagonal bowl, on a cylindrical stem raised upon two steps. The south porch is rude. The tower is large and coarse, with a battlement and flat-arched belfry window on each side, and slits for the other openings: at the north-east angle it has a staircase. The churchyard is very spacious, and contains some nice new gravestones in the form of crosses. There is but one bell.

LLANDDEWI BREFI (ST. DAVID).

July 5th, 1872.

This has been a church of much consideration, and belongs to an ancient college. The plan was cruciform, like Llanbadarn Vawr, but the transepts have been destroyed; the nave and chancel rebuilt in the most wretched style. Only the tower remains of the original structure: a massive plain one, of rather rude type, rising on four large plain pointed arches, opening to the nave, chancel, and transepts, of the rudest character, without any mouldings. The tower has a rude stone vault, open to the interior, without ribs. There is an embattled parapet and corbel table, and square turret at the north-east, rising above the parapet; the belfry windows oblong and square-headed. There is a door opening internally from the stair turret north of the chancel.

There is a silver chalice, thus inscribed: "POCVLVM ECCLIE DE LLANDDEWI BREFI, 1574"; the border rather pretty.

LLANYCHAIARN (ST. LLWCHAIARN).

A small church, scarcely worthy of notice, as the walls seem for the most part to have been rebuilt. It is merely a single small building, with a pointed bell-gable at the west end, containing an open arch and a rude western porch, having plain pointed doorways. The windows are all modernised. The font is small—an octagonal bowl on a stem set in a recess in the west wall.

TREGARON.

The body of this church is so modernised that it is doubtful whether any part of its walls is original; there is, however, a trace of an original stringcourse under the windows. There is neither chancel nor aisle. The tower is very rude and strongly built, and has a corbel table under the battlement, three stages of windows, and no buttresses.

The basement swells in dimension; on the north-east angle is a square stair-turret rising above the parapet. There is a west door and slight square-headed window above it, a belfry window similar, and a slit between them. The eastern belfry window is a flattened trefoil; the tower arch to the nave pointed and plain, springing straight from the walls.

(*To be continued.*)

NOTES ON THE OLDER CHURCHES IN THE FOUR WELSH DIOCESES.

BY THE LATE SIR STEPHEN R. GLYNNE, BART.

(*Continued from vol. xiv, p.* 307.)

DEANERY OF SUB AERON.

LLANARTH (ST. VYLLTYG).

August 19, 1859.

A church of rather higher pretension than most of its neighbours, yet very rude. It has a nave and chancel undivided, and a shallow chapel north of the latter, divided from it by a wide plain arch, and having a small square-headed slit on the west side.

The ground rises high on the north, and the north wall is quite low and has no windows, but one three-foiled lancet. The windows on the south and at the east end are modernised. The tower is solid and strongly built, the base spreads out, and there are no buttresses. The parapet embattled, with the forked Irish battlements, beneath which is a rude corbel table. There is a square turret at the north-east; belfry windows of two obtuse-headed lights, and the other openings mere slits. The doorway has a pointed arch; the tower arch is a plain pointed one. The interior is dreary and dark, but the width of the roof, with its plain open timbers, has not a bad effect. The font has a square bowl.

LLANDYSSUL (ST. TYSILIO).

June 25, 1855.

A large church, remarkable for Wales in having not only a tower but north and south aisles. In rudeness of architecture, however, it is hardly raised above the usual style of the neighbourhood.

The aisles are divided by arcades of very plain but tall pointed arches, having no moulding or ornament of any kind, with square piers of large size, without capitals. The Tower arch is similar. The chancel arch is of the same kind, but a modern plaster arch has been inserted within it. The windows are all of ugly modern Gothic design, except that at the east end, which is an original Perpendicular one of three lights. There is a plain stone shelf in the east wall. The chancel walls seem to have been rebuilt. The tower is a genuine rude Welsh one, strong and massive, without string or buttress, but with a battlement and corbel table, a west window, Perpendicular, of three lights, and square-headed belfry windows; a swelling base and square turret at the north-east. There is also a stone vault within the tower. The interior is pewed, but tolerably regular, and has a bare, frigid look. There is a huge pulpit with a sounding-board in the chancel arch. The font has a broken bowl, in shape like a quatrefoil, on a square base. There are modern monuments, and two inscriptions over family pews. One runs thus:—"This seat was erected at the expense of David Lloyd, Esq., and belongs to the House of Allt y Odyn in this parish by virtue of a faculty from the Bishop's Court."

A similar one to the house of Castle Howell. There are four bells. The churchyard beautifully situated, close to the Teivy on the north, with lovely view of its wooded banks; the graves marked out by pebbles in shape of coffins.

Llangranog (St. Caranog).

June 24, 1855.

A small church of common Welsh type, greatly modernised, situated on the declivity of a steep hill, and having the churchyard on the north, open to the hill. The walls low and whitewashed, no north windows—nor west—the others modern and wretched. There is a chancel arch of pointed form, but doubtful whether original. The belfry modern, and scarcely any vestige of original work to be seen.

Llanvihangel Ystrad (St. Michael).

September 11, 1847.

Plan, a body with north aisle and no marked chancel, no porch, an open belfry at the west; the whole glaring with whitewash. The arcade is formed by four very rude pointed arches with large wall piers, without mouldings or capitals. The font is attached to one pier, and has a square bowl, scolloped below, on a circular shaft set on two high steps. The windows are all modern. The eastern part which constitutes the chancel is boarded, the rest plastered. The whole is pued.

Llanwennog (St. Gwynog).

July 6, 1872.

A larger church than usual in this county; consists of nave and chancel, with a south aisle and a western tower. There is no chancel arch. The chancel is divided from the south chapel or aisle by two very rude pointed arches, considerably flattened, with no mouldings, and a large wall pier between them. There is no distinction of chancel. The windows appear to be rather Late, but some on the south of the nave of two lights have rather an Edwardian character. The east window is Perpendicular of three lights, some others have two plain pointed lights under a square head. The roof is coved throughout, and with ribs, but no bosses. The walls are very thick, and the whole has a solid character, rude, but not Early. The tower arch is a plain rude one, the tower has a stone vault, and is, as usual, without buttresses; has the swelling base, and a pointed west doorway, chamfered, with hood on head corbels. Over it is one stringcourse and a heraldic shield with portcullis, and another heraldic shield over the window. The west window is Perpendicular, of three lights. There are some slit-like openings, and belfry windows square-headed of two lights. At the north-east is a stair-turret rising above the parapet. The parapet is embattled, with corbel table below.

The font has a circular bowl on square stem, and is charged with odd-looking faces. The church is in good order, and nicely arranged, and has open seats; sacrarium laid with new tiles, and a good organ in the south chapel.

Aberporth (St. Cynwyl).

June 24, 1855.

A very small, mean church, so much dilapidated as to be entirely abandoned and condemned to be rebuilt. The plan is of the commonest and smallest Welsh kind: a diminutive body without distinction of chancel, and walls so low as to give it the air rather of a cottage. There is a western bell-gable, the windows modern, the roof open, and of not bad timber work. The west door pointed. In the north wall a sepulchral arch. All the fittings have been removed, and the service done in the adjacent school. The font has a rude square bowl, on a cylindrical stem and no base. The site lofty, remote from houses, with a fine view.

Llandyfriog (St. Dyfriog).

August, 1860.

This church is in a lonely spot close to the Teivy, consists of merely chancel and nave, and appears to have been mostly if not entirely rebuilt, though, perhaps, some of the old wall remains. But ancient architectural features have completely vanished. The chancel arch is nearly semi-circular, and probably modern, as are all the windows and internal fittings of the most ordinary character. There is the small single bell-gable at the west end, as usual in Welsh churches.

The view from the churchyard is very pleasant.

Penbryn (St. Michael).

August 23, 1869.

A neglected church, but ancient, consisting of nave and chancel, with a western porch and a bell-turret over the west end. The outer walls are whitewashed. The chancel arch is rather a rude pointed one, on imposts. The roofs have been modernised, as have all the windows of the nave. On the south of the nave near the east is a piscina. On the north side of the nave is a square-headed Perpendicular window of two lights, which are trefoliated. The church has one single lancet on the south, and one closed on the north. In the south wall of the chancel is a sepulchral arch. The porch is large, the doorway has rather a plain arch; the interior is dreary and ill-kept. The bell-gable has two open arches. The structure on a lofty eminence is fine, and commands a beautiful view of sea and land.

DEANERY OF EMLYN.

Clydai (St. Clydach).

August, 1860.

A larger church than the last (Kilrhedin, *inf.*, 357), gradually approaching the same state of ruin. It consists of nave and chancel, with south aisle extending along both, and western tower, all of the rude Welsh type, and probably of the Perpendicular period. The arcade is of four low and depressed arches, three in the nave and one in the chancel, with plain square piers. The western arch is particularly rude, the others have some sort of mouldings. The chancel arch is rude pointed.

There is a rood door set high up, and on the north is the projection for the staircase. The windows are all square-headed and Perpendicular, chiefly of three lights; some have fragments of stained glass. The tower is of very rude construction, is vaulted, and opens to the nave by a very coarse pointed arch. There is a ladder to the belfry storey, which opens to the nave by another pointed rough door. The tower is without string or buttress, is embattled, with slit openings and a rude door. The font is a rude circular cup, on a square base, chamfered. Everything is decayed and out of repair. There is a stoup by the south door. The outer walls are whitewashed. In the churchyard wall are some curious Early inscribed stones, noticed in *Archæologia Cambrensis*, 3rd Ser., vol. vi, p. 223, and 4th Ser., vol. v, p. 277.

KENARTH (ST. LLAWDDOG).

June 23rd, 1855.

The plan of this church is a nave and chancel, with south transeptal chapel. Over the west gable a bell-turret, with two open arches for bells. The church is long, and the ground rises, causing a considerable ascent towards the east. There is a plain pointed chancel arch, and a projection in the south wall. The windows all modern and very bad: no west windows, but a plain pointed door. The chancel and nave are both ceiled. The font is early, a square bowl with the common scalloping, the stem cylindrical; a cross on the east gable, and the outer walls whitewashed; the churchyard pretty and the graves flowered.

KILGERRAN (ST. LLAWDDOG).

June 23rd, 1855.

This church has lately been restored, and in great measure rebuilt, in a most creditable style unusual in the Principality. The walls seem to be entirely new, except the tower. The plan consists of nave, with south aisle, chancel, and western tower. The tower slightly tapers, and is of plain character, with small openings, a single cinquefoiled belfry window and no buttresses, a plain battlement. A west door has been added of greater pretension, of Early English character, with toothed mouldings and shafts; no west window. The arcade of the nave has three good pointed arches, with octagonal pillars, having capitals well formed of slate. The chancel arch is plainer and without imposts; the roof all open, and the seats uniform, low and open, and no gallery. The windows Decorated, of two lights, except those at the east end, which are of three, and filled with fair new stained glass in commemoration of two persons deceased. The east window of the south aisle is the best as to stained glass, in memory of —— Collis and his sister, Elizabeth Bearcroft. The chancel is stalled, and laid with encaustic tiles, the sacrarium more rich; the rails of iron, blue and gold. There are good crosses on the gables of the east end. The font is an imitation of that of St. Mary Magdalene, Oxford.

KILRHEDIN, PEMB. (ST. TEILO).

August, 1860.

This church has fallen into complete decay, so as to be unfit for divine service, and must soon be rebuilt. It has a nave and chancel, with a north chapel or aisle, which does not extend to the west end, but has at its west end a bell-gable for two bells, placed here instead of at the west of the nave. There are two wide flat arches, opening from the chapel to the body of the church, having an octagonal pier without capital. One of these arches is in the nave, the other in the chancel. The windows are all late Perpendicular and square-headed, of three lights, trefoiled and labelled, except one small single light on the north. The font has a square bowl, chamfered at the angles. There is a very great inclination in the chancel to the south. The bells bear the date 1754.

Llangeler.

August 5th, 1850.

This church is, like all its neighbours, whitewashed. It consists of a nave, with chancel, and a south chapel extending along the chancel, but only part of the nave. The division is formed by two rude pointed arches, with a rude square pier, having no mouldings. In the west gable are two open arches for bells. The south chapel has a square-headed east window, with label, of three lights without foils. Over the west door is a shallow niche. On the north side are some unsightly sash windows.

DEANERY OF KEMAES.

Nevern (St. Brynach).

August 3rd, 1850.

A large church in a lovely situation, in a richly-wooded valley, through which runs the Nevern river. It comprises a nave with south aisle, and a northern chapel, a long chancel, and a western tower. The form is rather irregular and the architecture rude, but it is a larger church than most others in the neighbourhood. There are two arches between the nave and the south aisle (which does not reach quite to the west) of very plain pointed form, with a rude square pier, and there is also a transverse arch across the aisle. The chancel arch is also pointed. The chancel is of fine proportions, and has both on the north-west and south-west a projection opening to the interior by flat arches in the thickness of the wall. On the north of the chancel is a two-light Middle Period window, and another similar one closed; also a Third Period one of two lights. Most of the other windows are debased and modernised with sashes. The tower is large but coarse, with a battlement and a square turret at the south-east; also a rough corbel table under the parapet. Most of the openings are slits: the belfry window is square-headed. Some of the tower is of slates, and there are buttresses at the west angles. There is a fine cross in the churchyard, which is most picturesque and lovely. (Engraved in *Arch. Camb.*, 3rd. Ser., vol. vi, p. 47).

LLANYCHAER (ST. DAVID).

July 9, 1872.

This church is fast hastening to decay, and presents

Llanychaer Church.

a sad spectacle. It consists of a nave and chancel, and a south aisle or chapel westwards joined on, and no steeple. The design is curious and the work extremely rude. The walls are very low, and over the west end is a bell-gable. There are no windows on the north, and the other windows have been mostly destroyed or modernised. The roof is dreadfully out of repair, the furniture ruinous, and the church disused save for funerals. There is a plain round arch between the nave and chancel, and a rude flat arch between the eastern and western divisions of the north aisle; between the channel and south aisle is no arch, but merely a flat beam.[1]

The Rev. T. G. Mortimer writes of this church:—

"The arch between the nave and chancel was pointed. The church was originally built in the form almost universal among the old churches of North Pembrokeshire: it consisted of nave, chancel, and south transept. There was a large hagioscope, or rather arched passage, from the transept to the chancel (as is still to be seen at Pontfaen). At a later period, another transept to the east of the original transept and touching it, was built—I imagine as a chapel for the family of Cilciffeth, who were very wealthy; that, however, must have been some centuries ago, as the family became extinct in the latter days of Queen Elizabeth, and the greater portion of the house itself, Cilciffeth, was then pulled down.

"Llanychaer church was rebuilt on the old foundations about twenty years ago (*c*. 1876). The eastern transept has now a lean-to roof; the other particulars are retained as far as form is concerned; but the chancel arch has been, I am sorry to say, made larger than it used to be; the arch between the transepts is retained."

ARCHDEACONRY OF CARMARTHEN—DEANERY OF LLANGADOCK.

Llandingat (St. Dingad).

May 14, 1851.

This church is just outside Llandovery town. It consists of a nave and chancel, each with south aisle, a western tower and north porch. The tower is of the rude Welsh kind, approaching castellated, without buttresses, with a battlement, below which is a billet cornice, a large square stair-turret at the north-east having slits for lights. The lower part of the tower, as usual, spreads out. The windows on the north side are mostly modern, those on the south square-headed and rather poor; the east window of the chancel square-

[1] Omitted in its proper place.

headed and small, of three lights; the north portion very large and plain. The doors pointed and simple. Over the porch a parvise, lighted by a slit. The arcade of the nave has three wide and entirely plain pointed arches, with large rude square piers. There are arches between the nave and chancel, and between the two south aisles, the former on octagonal piers, as is that between the chancel and south aisle. The organ is at the east end of the aisle. The outer walls, according to custom, are whitewashed. The font is modern; in the porch is a stoup.

Llanfair ar y Bryn.

May 14, 1851.

This church, about half a mile from the town of Llandovery, stands beautifully on a fine eminence and shaded with trees. It comprises only a nave and chancel, with south porch and west tower; the latter of a type very common in the district, without buttresses, embattled, with only one string-course. There is a rude billet cornice over the west doorway, but not under the parapet. At the south-east angle a square stair-turret with forked battlements. The belfry windows square-headed; that on the south has a flattened trefoiled head. The west window is a small one of two lights, plain Third Period; the other openings are merely slits. There is a modern excrescence on the north side. The porch is, as usual, very large, and contains a stoup. The chancel is not very well distinguished; the east window square-headed, of three lights. On the north of the chancel is a similar window of two lights, and a plain slit, also a door closed, probably connected with the rood-loft. The other windows are modern.

Llangadoc.

August 7, 1850.

This church has a nave and chancel, south transept, south porch, and west tower. The latter is very plain and coarse, without buttress or stringcourse, but having the common corbel table under the battlement. The openings are square-headed slits. The chancel arch is a rude pointed one. The roof is vaulted, but it is doubtful whether original and whether of stone. There are few windows, and those mauled and modernised. To the transept there is no arch. The church is pewed, and has a west gallery in a tolerably neat condition. The font has an octagonal bowl on a square pedestal. There are three bells.

Cayo (St. Cynwyl).

August 6, 1850.

This is rather a large rough church, consisting of two equal aisles and a west tower. The whole is very coarse, of Welsh character, and extremely solid, and what there is of architectural style is late and poor Third Perpendicular. The arcade dividing the aisles has four very rude pointed arches, with square piers of solid wall, having neither mouldings nor imposts. The eastern arch is at a wider interval. The east window is pointed, of three lights, and poor Third Perpendicular tracery; the others square-headed, of two and three lights, some labelled, and some not. The roof is coved and in very bad order, admitting the weather. The tower is extremely strong and solid; its arch to the nave is partly walled. The tower is embattled, without strings of division, and the masonry at the base spreads out wards. The belfry windows double, each obtuse-headed, but on the north single. Under the battlement is a corbel table. At the north-east is a square turret, the west door plain, and over it is a square-headed two-light window. The south door is labelled. The font is a small basin set in a recess on the south wall within the tower: a singular arrangement. The interior is out of repair; the tower vaulted within.

DEANERY OF UPPER CARMARTHEN.

CYNWIL ELVED.

June 22, 1855.

This church has a nave and chancel, with north aisle to both. The chancel is slightly divided, and extending a little to the east of the aisle: a bell-gable over the west end. There is a pointed west door. The north aisle does not reach quite to the west end. The arcade of the nave consists of two very wide obtuse arches, plain and rude, with a rough kind of octagonal pier. The font is attached to the pier, has an octagonal bowl on a stem of like form. There are very few windows on the north; some windows bad, with sashes, some plain Perpendicular, square-headed of three lights. There is a boarded coved roof to the north aisle, with embattled cornice: some windows of very plain character and square-headed. There is a tombstone to Thomas Howell, born 1676, died 1720. The chancel has one rude arch to the aisle, and a rude panelled boarded roof.

LLANGAN (ST. CANNA).

Sept. 15, 1856.

A small church of the single kind, without distinction of nave and chancel, and a pointed bell-cot over the west end; the whole of the exterior glaring from whitewash. There are no windows on the north, and those on the south are modern; the east window, square-headed, of two lights, and late character. The west door of very rude construction, but a pointed arch. The west end very bald, having no window. The nave has an open cradle roof, without bosses. The bell-cot has two arches, with bells. The south door is rude. The font is an irregular octagonal block of rude character. The interior is pued, but in neat condition. The churchyard is confined, and overcrowded with graves. The stones are very massive, but interspersed with evergreens and flowering plants.

DEANERY OF LOWER CARMARTHEN.

St. Clears.

October 23, 1845.

This church has a rude tower, a nave and chancel, without aisles. The tower of the common coarse style, without buttresses, but having a plain battlement and block cornice beneath it, and a square turret at the south-east angle. There are plain narrow square slits for the belfry and other apertures. The tower slightly tapers. On its west side is a rude arched door, and the lower part is vaulted in stone, as at Marros. The walls of this church lean outwards. The south doorway has an obtuse arch, set deeply in a very thick wall. The windows have been mostly mutilated. The chancel has a rude south door, with rather straight-sided arch, and no mouldings. On the south of the chancel is a quasi "lychnoscope": merely a square-headed aperture. The north door of the nave has an odd flat arch, but is closed. There is a Decorated window of two lights on the north side of the chancel. The west end of the nave is absurdly cut off from the remainder by a wooden partition, and a central passage formed through it from the tower, leaving a space on each side enclosed, used as a receptacle of rubbish—a very improper and unbecoming arrangement. The roof is open, with plain ribs. The chancel arch is a curious one, apparently of Norman character; the shape is segmental and depressed on the west side, presenting bold mouldings, and two orders of Norman shafts, with capitals of rude early foliage. On the east side there is no moulding and only plain imposts. On the north side of the nave, near the chancel arch, is a small obtuse window, set low, and now closed. The font has a circular bowl on a banded cylindrical stem, with square base. The church is pewed, and contains several ugly modern monuments. Part of the exterior is clothed with ivy.

Eglwys Cymmin (St. Margaret).

Sep. 3, 1861.

This church is of the same arrangement as Pendine, but in better order; and has, instead of a tower, a bell-cot over the west end, with one open arch for a bell. This seems to have been reconstructed of late years.

The church is remarkable for having a plain barrel vault stone roof to the nave. The chancel arch is small, rude and obtuse, set in a large mass of walling. There are no windows on the north of the nave; the other windows are new, and not happy imitations of Gothic; those on the south mostly square-headed, with labels. The new seats in the nave, though plain, are all open; the font new. The porch has an arched stone roof like the nave. The porch is large and coarse. The churchyard is very large.

Cyffig, or Kyffig.

June 19, 1869.

This church, distant two miles from Whitland Station, is in a lonely and rather picturesque site, and not easily found. It is a rude building, consisting of nave and chancel, with north aisle carried to the east end. There is a belfry gable at the west end of the nave for two bells, in open arches, and a large tower of the military rude type, at the west end of the aisle and engaged in it. There is a very rude arcade between the aisle and the body, which has three misshapen and irregular arches on plain square wall-piers. The first arch from the west is wide and pointed, the other two are much narrower. There is a rude arch opening to the tower. The chancel arch is a rude pointed one. The chancel is nearly equal in length to the nave. There is a plain pointed doorway at the west of the nave. The tower is probably of Perpendicular date, but having the local type; it is not easy to fix as to date. It has, however, a decidedly late Perpendicular doorway on the north, with Tudor arch and label; also a labelled square-headed window of like character. The tower has an embattled parapet and corbel table, but neither string nor buttress; the openings only narrow slits and square turret at the north-west, rising all the way. The few windows in the church have all been modernised.

Lampeter Velfrey (St. Peter).

August 20, 1869.

This church has been recently restored and is in very good order. It consists of two parallel aisles, without division, of which the northern terminates in chancel; a small north chapel and south porch, but no steeple. The arcade is formed by five pointed Early English arches, with plain soffits chamfered at the edge, on circular columns, having quasi-capitals, all of rather clumsy make. There is a plain pointed arch opening to the north chapel, in which is placed the organ. The windows seem to be wholly new, and are good Decorated, mostly of two lights, but of three at the extremities. The roof appears to be original, and has foliation above the collars. The east window has new coloured glass. There is a step ascending to the chancel. In the south aisle is a monument of the seventeenth century. The font has a square bowl, with the angles chamfered, on a square stem; The whole is fitted with open seats. The chancel has reredos and seats for the choir. The south doorway has a plain pointed arch. The porch is new.

Pendine.

Sept 2, 1861.

A small church, somewhat dilapidated; has only nave and chancel, a small western tower, and south porch. The latter has a rude pointed outer doorway, and within it a flat-topped doorway. There is a rude and small pointed arch between nave and chancel. On the north are no windows at all, and those on the south are mostly bad modern ones; but there is one small obtuse-headed one, now closed, on the south of the chancel. The east window is Decorated, of two lights. There is a small roofed projection both on the north and south, near the west end of the chancel. The font has an octagonal bowl on a circular stem. The tower is rude and small, without buttress or string-course, and has small slit-like openings. The east and west sides are gabled, so as to form a saddle-back roof. The churchyard is only to the south and east.

Llanddowror (St. Teilo).

July 1, 1867.

This church has been neatly rebuilt, except the tower, which is at the west end, and of the local type, much resembling the neighbouring one at St. Clear's. It is massive and strongly built, embattled, with corbel table under the battlement. Perpendicular belfry windows, square-headed of two lights, and a square turret at the south-east. The body of tolerable Gothic design, with nave and chancel.

DEANERY OF KIDWELLY.

Llanelly (St. Ellyw).

August 18, 1849.

A large church, much modernised, cruciform in plan, without aisles, and having a western tower. The latter is the only feature which preserves its original character, and is of the coarse Welsh kind, tapering and embattled, with thick walls, and the usual rude corbel table under the parapet. There are no buttresses, but a large square stair turret at the north-west. The belfry windows square-headed, with label. There is a modern west window and a plain pointed door. The chancel arch is a low pointed one. On the south side of the chancel is a single sedile (or piscina), with hood. Everything else, both within and without, is modernised, and in a very poor style. The east gable is surmounted by a cross. The font a plain octagon.

Pembrey (St. Illtyd).

June 20, 1855.

A large church of some interest and somewhat of the South Pembrokeshire make. The plan irregular, nave with north aisle. Chancel also with north aisle, and tower occupying the west extremity of the north aisle of the nave. There is also a bell-turret of the usual Welsh fashion, for two bells, in arches on the west gable of the nave, which looks as if the tower had been added afterwards. The tower much resembles those of Pembrokeshire and other parts of the south coast; but has forked battlements, tapering, without buttresses, and strongly built, with square turret at the north-east, and corbel table below the battlement. The belfry window square-headed. It has within a rude plain stone vault, and now forms a vestry in its lower part. There are two very wide and ill-shaped arches between the nave and aisle, of rude character, and without moulding. The pier octagonal, chamfered, without capital. Between the north aisle of the nave and that of the chancel is a rude pointed arch. The chancel has two rude arches dividing the aisle, the eastern pointed, the other round, with square chamfered pier. There is a rood door on the south of the chancel, and a shallow obtuse arch to the south of the altar; also a square basin for piscina. The chancel has been much modernised, especially in the windows: the windows of the north aisle are also bad. On the south is one Decorated one of two lights, and one late but handsome Perpendicular, one of four lights, with square head, which in its internal face presents much ornament; the rear arch moulded and has six shields, the central one charged with a cross, the other with armorial bearings as the portcullis of the Beaufort family; also a shield with three crosses in the earlier jamb, on a ledge. In the north aisle in the east wall is a rude stone shelf for an image. The roofs are open, and of cradle form. The south porch has a rude outer door, and there is a lych gate.

Archaeologia Cambrensis.

FIFTH SERIES.—VOL. XVII, NO. LXVI.

APRIL, 1900.

NOTES ON THE OLDER CHURCHES IN THE FOUR WELSH DIOCESES.

BY THE LATE SIR STEPHEN R. GLYNNE, BART.

(*Continued from vol. xv*, p. 369.)

DIOCESE OF BANGOR, ANGLESEY.

ABERFFRAW (ST. BEUNO).

September 16, 1848.

THIS church is double, consisting of two equal bodies without distinction of chancel, but the altar is at the east end of the southern aisle. There is a south porch and a gable belfry at the west end. There is an enriched Norman arch at the west end, having two orders and shafts with cushion capitals. The ornaments consist of chevron, and heads both human and animal; this arch is only seen inside the church, being blocked up externally. The south doorway within the porch seems to be First Pointed, with acute chamfered arch of two orders and imposts. The west end is graduated, and together with the bell-gable appears to be Jacobean. The rest of the church is late and poor, Third Pointed. The two east windows are of three lights, with a sort of Flamboyant tracery. Most other windows are square-headed, all without feathering, and some without arches. The roofs are poor and open, and there is a bit of inferior wood-carving in the cornice. The arcade consists of four bays, the arches wide, of Tudor form and chamfered; the piers have four clustered semi-octagonal shafts, with mouldings between them, and a general capital; the basis also octagonal. There is a break in the second pier from the west, which consists of a large piece of wall with shafts attached. The font has an octagonal bowl on a stem of the same shape, which is banded. The exterior is all whitewashed and the interior pewed. A north doorway is entirely plain.

Beaumaris (St. Mary).

This church is a neat building, far superior to the generality of Welsh churches. The plan is a western tower, a nave with side aisles and chancel, the whole of good and well-wrought stone; the nave, aisles, and chancel all embattled, and the latter enriched with pinnacles. The lower part of the tower has windows of lancet form, trefoiled; the upper story modern, of poor work, with a battlement of four plain pinnacles. The nave is divided from each aisle by four lofty, pointed arches, springing from octagonal pillars, above which is a clerestory with square-headed Perpendicular windows. The windows of the side aisles are chiefly Decorated, of two lights, but those at the east end of each Perpendicular. The chancel arch is pointed and plain. At the east end of the south aisle is an ogee canopied niche with crockets. The chancel is Perpendicular, the east window of five lights, with some portions of stained glass. On each side of the chancel are six wooden stalls, surmounted by fine canopies, and in the chancel is a fine alabaster altar-tomb, the sides enriched with figures and shields in niches, on which are the recumbent effigies of a knight and lady. On the north side of the chancel is a low chapel embattled, above which are set two square-headed windows lighting the chancel. On the south side of the altar is a stone commemorating Sir Henry Sydney and Sir Anthony St. Leger, Lords Deputies of Ireland, and others, erected by Edward Waterhouse, date 1565. There are several other inscriptions, and a modern white marble monument to Viscount Bulkeley. At the west end is this inscription :—

Here in their tender infancye
A brother and a sister lye,
One womb to them a being gave
And this same earth a resting grave.
Short was their race, but long their rest,
God soonest takes whom He loves best.

E. G. daughter of Rd. Gower, Gent., dyed 3 December, 1681.
W. G. son of the same, dyed 7 May, 1681.

The interior is, on the whole, neat and well-ordered. There is a good organ.

BODEDERN (ST. EDEYRN).

September 24, 1851.

This church is little superior in size or architecture to the generality of Anglesey churches, but it is in a neat and creditable state. It has only a single body, without division of chancel, and not even the common transeptal chapel. Over the west end the common arched bell-gable, restored, and on a larger scale than the older specimens. The church is entirely Third Pointed. The east window of three lights is pointed, and lately filled with painted glass, by Evans of Salop, in memory of the Rev. H. Wynne Jones. The other windows are square-headed, of two lights. The south doorway is of similar character, and labelled. The nave has an open roof; the chancel is ceiled. The west window is set high up in the wall. There is a modern screen between the nave and chancel. The font is an octagonal mass. The pews are neat and uniform, but closed.

CEIDIO.

September 24, 1851.

A very small church or chapel, like Gwredog (*infra*), only differing from it by the re-edification of the walls, which is done on the whole in a neat style, and the interior is very fairly arranged. The windows are square-headed and narrow. There is a new bell-cote at the west end for the bell. The east window is of two lights, of the Anglesey Flamboyant; the font a plain octagonal mass.

GWREDOG (ANGLESEY).

September 24, 1851.

This small chapel is of the Anglesey type, but from its diminutive size and the absence of burying-ground looks at a distance more like a house than a church. There is no chancel; at the west end is a small single bell-gable. The east window is a single one, trefoiled. The font is cylindrical on a square plinth. The roof is open, and there are very few windows. The altar as at Llantrisant.

HOLYHEAD (ST. CYBI).

September 17, 1848.

A more stately church than is usually found in North Wales. The plan is cruciform, the nave having aisles, with a western tower and a very fine south porch. The whole is late Third Pointed, and the south side of the nave much enriched. The tower is extremely plain and coarse, and is not square, the sides being unequal. It has a battlement, but no distinctive architectural feature. The aisles, porch, and transept are all embattled. The east side of the south transept has its battlement pannelled and enriched with curious figures of animals and legends of saints, but at the south end this battlement is interrupted. The battlement of the north transept is plainer. The buttresses of the south aisles are crowned with pinnacles, but they have been broken on the north side. The windows of the aisles

Holyhead Church. View from the South-East.

are of three lights; in the south aisle they have foliations. The clerestory windows are of two lights, and square-headed; two modern ones are added at the east end of the nave over the arch. At the east end of the south aisle is an octagonal stair-turret, with a pyramidal finishing and quatrefoiled cornice. The chancel has also three-light windows, somewhat depressed. On the north side of the chancel is an appearance of an obtuse lychnoscope. The nave has internally on each side an arcade of three Tudor-shaped arches, having moulded hoods on angel figures bearing shields. On the north, the piers are octagonal; on the south, clustered of four shafts, with general capital. On the south, the corbels of the hoods are unfinished. The roof is flat and low-pitched, with a few bosses. The arrangement of the transept is odd and clumsy, like other instances in North Wales, running from north to south uninterrupted by arches, and giving the effect of one church being set at right angles to another; yet the nave opens to the transeptal space by a Tudor arch and the chancel by another, but the usual effect of a crossing is lost. The chancel has been greatly modernised, but the church is altogether in a neat and decent condition. The organ is in the north transept. The south porch is much the finest feature about the church. It has three-light windows on each side, the tracery of which is continued below them. The battlement is flanked by pinnacles. The outer door has shafts and looped quatrefoiled spandrels. The inner door is very rich, of Tudor form, labelled, with fine mouldings enriched with foliage and panelled spandrels. Above it is a large piece of panelling of great beauty, with several distinct bands containing loops, quatrefoils, etc., and in the centre a niche, with rather depressed crocketed canopy, having shafts, and in the spandrels foliage and shields. The forms and general character are late. The groining has never been finished. The churchyard is surrounded by an ancient wall.

Llanallgo (St. Allgo).

April 24, 1868.

This church is less altered than most of those of Anglesey, and is of a rather singular form, having a kind of cruciform plan; the western arm or nave is remarkably short, the northern and southern are rather disproportionate transeptal chapels, and the eastern is a decided chancel. The walls are very low, and over the west gable rises a rude bell-cot formed with one arch. At the west end externally is a stone ledge, as seen elsewhere in Anglesey. There is no chancel arch, nor yet to the chapels. The chancel roof is open and of cradle form, the rest ceiled. The west window is modern and bad. The south transept end has a Perpendicular square-headed labelled window of two lights. On the east side of each transept is a single window, that of the northern having foliation. There is no window in the nave. Part of the rood-screen remains. The east window of the chancel is a very good one of Perpendicular tracery of three lights, and contains portions of good coloured glass. On the south of the chancel is a square-headed labelled Perpendicular window of two lights. The font has a plain circular bowl, raised on steps. The church is out of order, and needs repair; the interior very rough. The pulpit is at the west end. In the churchyard is a monumental stone, recording that one hundred and forty bodies were buried in the churchyard from the wreck of the *Royal Charter*, and forty in that of the adjoining parish of Penrhos Llugwy.

Llanbadrig (St. Patrick).

October 5, 1849.

A plain church, with scarcely any remarkable features, though a remote antiquity has been assigned to it. It is long and narrow, without aisles, having a south porch and a bell-gable at the west end. The east window is a poor one, of three lights and late character;

all the others are modern and wretched. The porch has a stoup in one angle. The chancel arch is obtuse and rude. A large part of the western portion of the nave is separated for a school, and the pews are modern. The porch is very near the west end. The churchyard is uneven, and overhangs the sea in a romantic way.

LLANBEDR GOCH (ST. PETER).

December 15, 1849.

The plan cruciform, without aisles; the transepts, as usual, awkward and sprawling, advancing near to the east end, and much out of proportion to the short chancel and insignificant nave. There is a single arched belfry at the west gable. The walls are low. A north door is late Third Pointed, with label and panelled spandrels. The windows few, mostly square-headed and debased, but that at the east end is Middle Pointed, of three lights, late in the style, and of a character very frequent in Anglesey. There is no west window. The roofs are of plain timber framework, and no arches to the chancel or transepts. The font a plain octagon. The situation of this church is on an abrupt rocky eminence.

LLANDEGVAN (ST. TEGVAN).

December 14, 1849.

An interesting church, much modernised; in form a clumsy cross, with modern west tower, built 1811, and a south porch. There are but few original features remaining. The windows all modern ones. The roofs are plain and barn-like; the chancel very small, and not separated by an arch. There are, however, two awkward stone arches thrown across the north transept. The latter is raised up two steps, as is the chancel, on account of the uneven ground. In the north transept against the east wall is a modern Gothic monument. No font could be found.

LLANDDEUSANT (ST. MARCELLUS).

September 24, 1851.

A small church, of the Anglesey type, with nave and chancel and western bell-gable. The chancel is divided from the nave by a rude and obtuse arch, rising upon imposts. The east window is Middle Pointed, of three lights, the western one a single obtuse-headed light, set high up. Other windows are square-headed and debased, or else modern wretched insertions, and there seem to have been none originally on the north. There are north and south doors, with obtuse heads. The roof is of an ordinary kind. There is a kind of cupboard in the north wall of the nave. The font is cylindrical. The pulpit and desk, according to a Welsh fashion, flank the altar.

LLANDDONA (ST. DONA).

December 15, 1849.

A curious church, having north and south transepts clumsily developed, but with the addition of a diminutive aisle or chapel on the south of the nave, adjacent to the transept, but not continued quite to the west. There is a north porch, and a small western bell-gable for one bell. The walls are low; there is no west window, but a plain door. The porch is very large, and Third Pointed of late character. The inner door has a very obtuse arch, with mouldings and panelled spandrels. A singular effect is produced within from there being a pointed arch across the nave near its western part, dividing it into two parts, and not separating the chancel. The small aisle has one plain, low, pointed arch, opening to the nave, but its western bay has no arch, only a wooden upright pier. The font stands against this pier: a plain octagonal bowl on two steps. The prevailing features are early Third Pointed, but some are later. The north transept has a window of two lights without foils, and very rude, apparently

Middle Pointed, and resembling one at Brownsover in Warwickshire. The chancel is very short, the transepts, as usual in Anglesey, reaching near to the east end. The roof of the chancel is plastered. There is a rude low pointed arch between the chapel and the south transept, as well as the nave. The east window is square-headed, and very late Third Pointed, neither labelled nor foliated. There is the date 1590 on a stone above it. There are scarcely any windows on the south, but a loop on the south of the sacrarium. The gables have been all capped by crosses, but only that on the north transept remains. The situation is sequestered and pleasing, near the Traeth Coch. The ground of the churchyard rises eastwards.

LLANDDYFNAN (ST. DYFNAN).

November 22, 1865.

This church has nave and chancel only, and a south porch with a small bell-cot over the west end. The walls have been for the most part rebuilt. The chancel arch is pointed, very poor and meagre. There are late square-headed windows in the chancel at the east end, of three lights, the others of two; the south-east window set under a flat-pointed arch in the wall. The windows are labelled externally. There is a modern addition at the west end, looking like a narthex, and opening by a pointed arch. The south porch is large, and has trefoil-headed windows on the sides. The outer doorway has a pointed hood. The north doorway has also a hood-moulding upon corbels, sculptured with very curious figures of animals. Over it is a bust with lifted hands. Near this door is a stoup. The font has a plain octagonal bowl. The seats are mostly open and new.

LLANDYSILIO (ST. TYSILIO).

January 27, 1850.

This very small church is a well-known object to those who have frequented the Menai Bridge: seated on a rock nearly surrounded with the water of the Menai, and accordingly difficult of access, and remote from the population of the parish. It has very low walls and no distinct chancel, a small single bell-gable over the west end. There is a north door, but none on the south or west, and very few windows except at the east end, where is one of the transition kind, Middle to Third Pointed, so frequent in Anglesey, and of three lights. No windows at all on the south. The roof is open, and though rude not bad of its kind. The interior dark ; part of the screen remains parting the chancel, but not of any decided character. The font a plain octagonal basin.

Llanedwen (St. Edwen).

May, 1850.

A very small church in a lovely situation, shaded with trees, and commanding a beautiful view over the Menai. There is no distinction of nave and chancel ; the windows are square-headed, except the eastern, which is pointed, and has no tracery. The font is cylindrical. Over the west end is an open-arched belfry for one bell. There is a square-headed slit window on the south of the chancel.

Llaneilian (St. Eilian).

October 5, 1849.

A curious church, superior to the generality in the county, consisting of a lofty but not long nave ; a chancel of lower elevation, a south porch, western steeple, and a singular chapel on the south of the chancel, but not in a right line with it, and approached by a low passage. The nave is fair Third Pointed, of good stone, and more finished than is usual. The chancel also Third Pointed, rather plainer ; the chapel has some earlier indications, but no part of this church can approach to the age which is assigned to it, as it is supposed a church was founded here first in the fifth century. The nave is embattled, with the buttresses crowned by pinnacles; the porch is plain, the interior door having good continuous mouldings; in one of its angles is a stoup. The north door has also tolerable mouldings. The chancel is lower than the nave, but has also a battlement and pinnacles. There is an octagonal stair-turret at the south-east angle of the nave, communicating with the roof, and also with the rood-loft. The roofs are leaded. The windows of the nave are of three lights. The interior would have a good effect if it were better fitted up, the elevation of the nave being considerable, but it is too short. The tower arch is an obtuse one, upon imposts; that to the chancel pointed, upon octagonal shafts. There is a rude rood-screen, with coarse cornices of fruit and foliage above and under the panelling of the loft, the screen itself rather plain. The west gallery exhibits some wood screen work with the date 1533. Some of the benches are open, but very plain. The chancel has square-headed windows of two lights; the eastern one of three resembles a triple lancet in some degree, but is most probably Third Pointed. It contains some Third Pointed stained glass. The original stalls and desks remain, with coarse poppy-heads, and are of a plain sort. The altar is a large carved chest of wood, inscribed with "Non nobis Domine," with the date 1634. The roofs of both nave and chancel are low-pitched, that of the chancel most ornamental, having flowered bosses and figures of a grotesque sort supporting the spandrels, having wigs, and playing musical instruments. The crooked passage which leads from the chancel to the south chapel is lighted by small square-headed windows. The chapel has an east window of Middle Pointed character of two lights; on the south a square-headed one without foils. The roof is plain, and the parapets embattled. At the point of the west gable is an arch for a bell. Against the east end is a curious kind of altar, hexagonal in form, of wood, and appearing also to have formed a respository for vestments, with open panels in front. In the east wall is a recess and a ledge, also an arched recess in the west wall. The roof of this chapel has moulded beams. The steeple has a curious appearance, and is constructed oddly of slates, the tower in three stages diminishing, and surmounted by a heavy four-sided spire, also of slate, and occupying the entire square. The openings of the steeple are plain single lights. There are three bells; the font is modern. Close to the north door is a large poor-box, covered with iron-work. There is a cross on the south side of the churchyard.

Llanfachreth.

July 16, 1873.

The church has merely nave and chancel, small and undivided, with a small Welsh bell-gable over the west end. The east window is remarkable, of two lights, and of a sort not uncommon in Anglesey, the two lights trefoiled, and in the upper part a lozenge, from the higher point of which is a straight line to the top of the arch. The other windows mostly of obtuse-headed lights; one on the south is labelled; there is none at the west end. The south doorway is rude, and has a semicircular arch on imposts, almost like Norman. Under the east window externally is a stone ledge, and above its apex is a rude head. The interior is mean and pewed.

Llanfaes (St. Catherine).

December 15, 1849.

This church appears to have been almost wholly rebuilt within the last three years, and presents an appearance of some elegance; a new tower having been erected, surmounted by a broach spire of very good execution, quite a rare feature in Wales. The church has a nave and chancel, divided by a continuous pointed arch. The east windows Middle Pointed, of three lights, filled with fair modern stained glass, the other windows, square-headed, in the same style. In the north porch is an octagonal stoup. The interior fittings are neat, and the situation very pretty.

Llanfair Pwllgwyngyll (St. Mary).

May 24, 1850.

A very small church, the walls so low that it is with difficulty distinguished; but the situation, near to the shores of the Menai, is very pretty. There is only a nave and chancel, which latter is remarkable for a semicircular apsidal termination, which is very rude, and apparently of early Norman work. It opens westward by a rude misshapen arch on imposts, and in its north pier is a square hagioscope; there is also some appearance of the beginning of a stone vault. The altar is set lengthwise, and much encroached on by pews and rails, the more inexcusable from the peculiar arrangement. There are no original windows; those which there are, are square-headed and debased. There is a plain-pointed arched bell-gable over the west end for the bell. There is no west door nor window; the only door is on the north, near which is a rude early cylindrical font. In the churchyard has been erected a columnar tombstone, rising higher than the roof of the church, in memory of several workmen and others employed in the construction of the Britannia Bridge, who lie buried here.

Llanfair-ynghornwy (St. Mary).

September 4, 1867.

This is one of the large churches of Anglesey, and consists of a long nave, a chancel with large chapel on the south, and a western tower. The south porch is made into a vestry. The whole is Perpendicular, but the south chapel of the latest type, divided from the chancel by three flat Tudor arches on octagonal pillars, and the windows are of corresponding character. There is one window, south of the nave, of two lights with trefoil heads. The east window of the chancel is a very good Perpendicular one of three lights, early in the style. There is no chancel arch, but there is a wood screen across the chancel, the roof of which is open with plain rude timbers. The chancel is fully equal to the nave in length. The tower is rude and plain, with battlement, and one stringcourse and six buttresses. There is an open bell-arch in the parapet on the west side, as at Llanerchymedd. On the west side is a pointed doorway, tall, and with face-mouldings. The churchyard is secluded, and shaded by fine trees.

Llanfechell (St. Mechell).

September 4, 1867.

This church is rather a large one for North Wales, and consists of a nave with south transept, chancel, west tower, and south porch. The south doorway within the porch has a Norman character, with plain semi-circular arch on imposts. The south chapel or transept opens to the nave by a plain pointed arch; the nave has an open roof, with arched timbers; the transept is vaulted in stone, and has some Decorated windows, in which appear pieces of coloured glass with heraldic shields (and arms of Bulkeley), and a figure of St. Machutus. Some other windows of the nave are plain late Perpendicular. There is no chancel arch. There is a single lancet south of the chancel; the east window of three lights has something of the Anglesey Flamboyant character. The tower is a late addition against a solid west wall; it is built in a plain and solid manner, without buttresses, having three string-courses below the battlement, and the only opening is a small slit; the only door is from within. Upon it is a small octagonal spire of stone, with ribs at the angles. The font is square, on each side having two rude Norman arches with imposts.

LLANFFLEWIN (ST. FFLEWYN).

September 4, 1867.

A small church, with low walls, and undivided, with a pointed bell-cot over the west end, with an open arch. The church has been so completely modernised, that it is doubtful whether any original feature remains but the bell-gable and one single-light window in the north wall. All other windows are modern. The font is of singular design—octagonal, swelling downwards, and each face concave. The seats open. The site is wild and striking.

LLANFIHANGEL DIN SILWY (ST. MICHAEL).

August 3, 1859.

The church has been for the most part rebuilt. It has nave and chancel, with neat modern bell-cot. The chancel arch is pointed, and very plain, of the original work. The east window is Decorated, of three lights, with hood on head corbels, and on the south of the chancel is one of Perpendicular character, with square head. Other windows are modern. On the east gable is a good cross. From the churchyard is a very fine view. There is a pretty carved moveable pulpit of wood.

LLANFIHANGEL YSCEIFIOG (ST. MICHAEL).

November 22, 1865.

The old church having been abandoned, and a new one built in the village of Gaerwen, only a small portion of it now remains, and that in a dilapidated state, and in a remote situation. The church had originally a nave with aisle and a chancel with a north chapel; but only the chancel with the chapel now remain, and the west end of the chancel is walled, and has inserted a good Perpendicular doorway, brought from some other part of the church, which has good mouldings and spandrels, with quatrefoiled circles. The original small bell-cot has also been removed to this place. The interior presents a wretched scene of decay. Between the chancel and the north chapel is no arch, but merely a flat kind of entablature. This chapel is of debased character, and has a square-headed window of three lights, also a late doorway with flattened arch. Some woodwork bears the date 1684. Some of the old benches still remain, with round ball-like heads of the bench ends.

LLANFWROG (ST. MWROG).

July 16, 1873.

There is a nave and chancel, with south porch and new pointed bell-cot over the west end. The whole is very much renovated; indeed, apparently rebuilt. The windows have mostly Perpendicular tracery of three lights; at the west end is one square-headed with two ogee lights more like Decorated. The east window is transitional to Perpendicular, and some others are of both sorts. The font has a plain octagonal bowl. There is no west window; the vestry new, and the whole in fair condition.

LLANGADWALADR (ST. CADWALADR).

September 12, 1848.

A church of low pitch, with nave and chancel only, but with the singularity of a debased Gothic chapel on the south side of the chancel; there is also a hideous modern one on the north, built in 1801: also a south porch. Over the west end is a bell-gable, with three open-pointed arches, each containing a bell. The porch has stone benches, and the inner door has a flattened head, upon which is an inscription; "Catamanus Rex;"[1] within the porch is a benatura with three-sided basin. There is a north door, which has a moulding and impost of curious appearance, resembling First Pointed, now glazed. There is no west window. On the south of

[1] "Catamanus Rex sapientisimus opinatisimus omnium regum." —*Arch. Camb.* ii, 166.

the nave is a late square-headed one of two lights; other northern windows are debased. The east window of the chancel is a very fair Middle Pointed one of three lights, with moulded hood, and rather verging to Flamboyant. In it is some stained glass, in which may be deciphered "Orate pro bono statu-ap-armigeri." In the centre the Crucifixion, and several canopied figures of saints. The roof of the nave is open, the beams forming flat arches on foliated timbers which form brackets. The chancel is very obtuse, and seems to have been altered. Across it is a plain Italian wood screen. The font has an octagonal bowl, upon a pedestal of like form. The south chapel is a curious specimen of its age. It is embattled, with a gable flanked by points and terminated by a fleur-de-lys. On the west side a door with graduated label, and very small window by the side. On the south a four-light window with transom flanked by buttresses, and on each side of it a small square-headed one of two lights. At the east end is a similar window, of which the transom is embattled. The church is fitted with open benches, except the two chapels, which are pewed. In the north chapel are some ugly monuments, some of Elizabethan style. The south chapel has a boarded roof, painted in bad style. Tower built by Aron Owen in 1661, as an inscription shows.

Llangoed (St. Cawrdaf).

August 3, 1857.

This church is quasi-cruciform, having north and south transeptal chapels set very near to the east end. The church is low, and long in proportion. The chancel arch a plain-pointed one, springing at once from the wall. Over the debased east window is the date 1613. There is a kind of hagioscope from the north chapel into the chancel. The north transept reaches further east than the chancel. The form is very anomalous. The south pier of the chancel arch stands, as it were, insulated in the south chapel. There are square-headed Perpendicular windows in the south transept; the north transept is more debased in style. There is a stone block at the south-west corner of the transept. The whole of the interior is out of repair, with most irregular pews. The pulpit is a fair carved one, of wood on stone base. The altar is all but squeezed out of its place by pews. The font has an octagonal bowl on a stem. There is a small open bell-cot for one bell.

LLANGRISTIOLUS (ST. CRISTIOLUS).

October 27, 1849.

A fair specimen of the better sort of Anglesey village church, consisting of nave and chancel without aisles, but of good proportions, and the chancel properly distinguished and developed. A south porch and single-arched belfry over the west end. The chancel arch is of considerable elegance, unusual in North Wales, having excellent moulding and clustered shafts which have a Middle Pointed character. The east window is of five lights and Third Pointed, the other windows of similar period, but square-headed. The cill of the south-east window is extended as for a sedile. The porch has a good outer door, with mouldings in the soffit. There is a priest's door on the south of the chancel, and on the south side of the division, between nave and chancel, is a projection which seems a continuation of the east gable of the nave. The interior is neat.

LLANGWYFAN.

September 5, 1863.

This church is chiefly remarkable for its situation upon a rock surrounded at high tide by the sea-water, but at low tide approached by a rough causeway. It is of the usual Anglesey make, without distinction of chancel, and with low walls and a bell-gable at the west for one bell. There has, however, once been a north aisle the whole length of the church, and the arcade of three very low and wide Tudor arches on short octagonal pillars may be seen in the wall. The east window, of two lights, has rather an early Decorated look ; one window on the south is Perpendicular, of a single-light, cinquefoiled and labelled, and one on the north is somewhat similar. The porch is plain ; within it a late Perpendicular doorway with label and panelled spandrels. The interior is rude, the seats are mostly on one side—some open—some pews, much crowding upon the altar. Against the south wall internally is a stone bench ; the roof open. The font has a plain octagonal bowl on a stem ; there is no west window.

LLANIDAN (ST. AIDAN).

May, 1850.

The old parish church, now abandoned and in great measure ruinated, is in a secluded site close to Lord Boston's house. It is a larger and better structure than most of the Anglesey churches. It consists of two equal aisles, divided by an arcade of Tudor arches, with octagonal piers. The western portion is still roofed, and used for funerals, but the larger part of the church is open to the skies. There are some Middle Perpendicular indications, but most of the windows are square-headed. The porch has a plain stone vault, and contains a stoup. Over the west end is a bell-gable with one bell in an arch, and mantled with ivy ; the font is cylindrical.

LLANSADWRN (ST SADWRN).

August 31, 1871.

A small church of the local type, having nave and chancel, and a chapel or transept clumsily set in the north and coming near to the east end. The church has lately been restored and put into decent condition. The walls are very low, the windows square-headed, of late character, save that of the east end, which is of two lights, and Decorated character; but all seem to have been renovated. There is no arch to the transept, but the timbers of the roof are clumsily arranged. Over the west end is the original bell-cot, having pointed gable and open arch for bell.

Llantrisant (SS. Avian, Ieuan, and Sanan).

September 24, 1851.

This church has a nave and chancel, with large disproportionate south chapel or transept, which ranges with the east end of the chancel. The walls are very low, and there is the usual single-arched gable for a bell at the west end. The windows are all bad except the eastern one, which is plain Third Perpendicular, of two lights. The south doorway has a debased look, with a very obtuse arch and label over it. The interior is tolerably neat, but the altar is as usual closely encumbered by pews. The altar itself is at right angles with the east wall. The font is early, probably Norman; the bowl cylindrical, sculptured with a kind of scroll-work with rude foliage, and upon a square plinth. At the east end of the transept is a square aperture near to the ground.

Llanynghenedl.

July 16, 1873.

A small church, with very low walls, and bell-cot for one bell over the west end. There are some small rude windows, with obtuse heads, single and double. The roof the nave is open, that of the chancel boarded. The north door has pointed arch in wood, trefoil-headed. The south door has obtuse head; there is no west window.

NEWBOROUGH (ST. PETER).

September 12, 1848.

Rather a curious church, comprising a nave and long chancel, with a south porch and a gable belfry over the west end, having two pointed open arches for bells. There is rather more variety of architecture than usual in Welsh churches. The porch has a good open timber roof. Though there is a long architectural chancel, it does not seem to have been used entirely as such, but only the east portion, which is separated by a broken wood screen; and the west part of the nave is now partitioned off and not used, so that the internal effect does not answer to the unusually long exterior. The east window is Middle Perpendicular, of three lights, with hood on head-corbels. On the south of the original chancel are two tolerable windows, also Middle Perpendicular, of two lights, the rear arch having good bold mouldings. There is one lancet on the north of the nave, and one with trefoil-head at the west; the other windows are chiefly square-headed and late, some debased. The door within the porch is of depressed form. The interior is very shabby in appearance; the benches are old, but quite rude and plain. The font is curious and early; it is a cylindrical mass, sculptured with interlacing ornament and some figures resembling a Greek cross. Under the south-east window is what appears a sedile and a piscina. The priest's door has a hood, with corbels.

The situation of this church is so elevated that it is seen at a great distance, both in Carnarvonshire and Anglesey.

PENMON (ST. SEIRIOL).

This church is cruciform, without aisles, having a tower in the centre, with pointed roof of stone. The whole is of Norman origin, and the nave now disused. The south door has a good semicircular arch, with embattled moulding upon shafts; the door itself has a square head, and above it, in the head of the arch, is some rude sculpture, in which is seen the figure of a lion. The north door has a flattened trefoil head. There are small round-headed windows set high in the wall, and some flat buttresses. The tower is finished by a rude pointed roof of rough stones overlying each other, and has in the belfry story double windows with a central shaft of rough and simple construction. The tower rises upon arches, of which the south and west are semicircular of rather good ornamental character, having billet and chevron mouldings and shafts, with abaci and varied capitals. The eastern arch is semicircular, but much plainer. The north transept is destroyed. In the south transept under the windows is a range of Norman arches springing from shafts, with abaci to the capitals, and having chevroned mouldings. In the chancel is a Perpendicular window, and on the south of the altar a plain niche and an ambry in the east wall. The south transept is open to a plain roof, and adjoining it is a part of the monastic buildings now occupied as a farm-house. On the south of the chancel was the refectory, now ruinated and finely mantled in ivy. Its character is Perpendicular. The font is square, with a bunch of cushion capital. From this church is a fine view of Penmaen Mawr.

Penmynydd.

October 26th, 1849.

A neat little church, consisting of a nave and chancel, a small shed-like chapel on the north of the nave, and a south porch. Over the west end, an arched gable for two bells. The chancel is properly developed, and divided from the nave by a pointed arch, which springs from semi-octagonal shafts. A low arch opens from the nave to the north chapel, which is low and narrow, but contains a fine altar-tomb. The windows are mostly square-headed, of two lights, also Third Pointed. The east window of three lights, also Third Pointed; the lateral ones of the chancel are single, and on the south is a priest's door. The west window is a fair Third Pointed one of three lights, with small embattled transom across the central light. The south porch has stone benches; on the door some good ironwork. There are crosses on the gables; the roof newly slated; the interior very neat and creditable, fitted with open benches having poppy-heads. In the churchyard is a small shaft of a cross.

PENRHOS LLUGWY (ST. MICHAEL).

April 24, 1868.

This church has been almost wholly rebuilt, and has a very neat, creditable appearance. Possibly some of the walls are original, but there is no certain appearance of old work. It has nave and chancel; the chancel arch new; as also all the windows, save the eastern, which is good Decorated of two lights; the others are of rather Flamboyant character. The seats are all open. Over the west end is a new bell-cot, with bell in an open arch. The font is old, the bowl octagon, having a kind of shallow battlement at each angle in the upper part. The base is very rude.

PENTRAETH (ST. MARY).

October 6, 1849.

This church has the usual Welsh arrangement of nave and chancel undivided, and a large transeptal chapel on the south; a south porch and western bell-gable. The east window is a fair Middle Pointed one of three lights; most of the other windows late and square-headed, some debased. In the roof of the nave, on the south side and near the west end, is a dormer window which appears ancient. The roof of rude timber framework, but over the sacrarium boarded. In the east wall is a trefoil-headed niche. The font is a rude octagonal block, set on square plinth and steps. The church has been newly pewed. The situation is pretty, and surrounded by trees.

RHOSCOLYN (ST. GWENVAEN).

December 18, 1856.

A small church of the common Anglesey make, in rather a commanding situation, not far from the romantic cliffs which present such splendid appearances and geological curiosity. It has merely a nave and chancel without divisions, a south porch, and pointed Welsh bell-cot at the west end for two bells. The porch has its outer door, with continuous mouldings of late character. Within the porch is a fair Perpendicular, door with label and panelled spandrels. The east window is of two lights, and probably Perpendicular, though having a Decorated look like some others in the island. On the south is a square-headed single window, cinquefoiled. The other windows are modern. The roof of the nave is open and of cradle form ; that of the chancel ceiled. The font is curious and Perpendicular, the bowl octagonal, charged with varied panelling or other figures on each face, and the patterns being continued down the stem, which is raised on two steps. The chancel is crowded with pews, and has a large west gallery, but is on the whole clean and decent. The churchyard rather small and confined.

TAL-Y-LLYN (ST. MARY).

July 3, 1872.

A small and mean church, with a general resemblance to many in Mona. It has nave and chancel only, with a chapel on the south of the latter. There are no windows on the south, except one closed. On the north are two bad modern ones ; at the east, a late Perpendicular one of three lights, square-headed and labelled, with no foliation. The west doorway has an obtuse arch, with rather deep mouldings, probably late

Perpendicular. There has been a chancel arch of Tudor form, partially closed; there is a mean bell-cot at the west end. The font is an oblong, two sides bearing a rude cross; the others plain.

TREFDRAETH.

October 27, 1849.

This church has a nave and chancel undivided, a large chapel on the south of the chancel, and a south porch. At the west end, an arched gable for one bell. There is no chancel arch; the chapel on the south resembles several others in a similar situation in Anglesey and Carnarvonshire, and ranges with the east end. It is late Third Perpendicular, having a labelled door in its west side, and opens to the chancel by a pointed arch, across which a lower one is thrown. The east window is in the Perpendicular, of three lights, rather singular in tracery, and with something of a Flamboyant character. The lights are cinquefoiled. The windows are mostly square-headed, labelled, and of two lights, of a late date; one on the south has coarse head-corbels attached to the label.

There is a new slate roof; the situation high, within a very large cemetery, and commanding an extensive view; the seats mostly open and plain.

(*To be continued.*)

Archaeologia Cambrensis.

FIFTH SERIES.—VOL. XVII, NO. LXVII.

JULY, 1900.

NOTES ON THE OLDER CHURCHES IN THE FOUR WELSH DIOCESES.

BY THE LATE SIR STEPHEN R. GLYNNE, BART.

(*Continued from* p. 109.)

DIOCESE OF BANGOR.

CARNARVONSHIRE.

ABER (ST. BODFAN).

THIS church has a modern west tower, a nave, south transept, and chancel. There is not much that is remarkable in it. The windows are chiefly square-headed, of two lights, and late Perpendicular, and two are of three lights. The transept has the rude open timber roof so common in Wales. There is some pretty good wood-carving, now incorporated in a pew, and some neat open seats. The font has a plain octagonal bowl, on a cylindrical stem.

ABERDARON (ST. HYWYN).

September 19, 1849.

The old church, now forsaken and left to fall to ruin[1] (a new one having been built, in another situation), is one of the best in the county; consisting of the usual

[1] It has been partially restored for service.

Welsh arrangement of two equal aisles (a nave, with undistinguished chancel, and parallel north aisle), with a bell-cot over the gable of the aisle. The whole is late Third Pointed, except a plain Norman door at the west end of the north aisle, and a small window, now almost closed, on the north side, near the east end. The doorway has three orders, with imposts, but no shafts. There are no windows at all on the north side, except the small one noticed. The other windows are of three lights, except that at the east end, which is of five, with a transom. The nave is divided from the aisle by an arcade of five Tudor-shaped arches, with mouldings, springing from octagonal pillars. The roof is open, and a fair specimen of a Welsh one: the timbers on stone brackets. There is a stone bench along the east end of the north aisle, some open benches, and a part of a poor late rood-screen. The font has an octagonal bowl, on a stem of like form. Part of the west end is used as a school. The churchyard closely adjoins the sea-shore.

Abererch (St. Cowrda).

July 16, 1850.

A larger church than most of those in the neighbourhood, all late Third Pointed. It consists of a nave and chancel undivided, with a north aisle reaching along both, but not extending quite to the west end of the nave. There is the usual open-arched belfry at the west end. The arcade has two bays in the chancel, and two in the nave, the break between them being a large wall-piece. The arches are Tudor-shaped and depressed, the piers octagonal, with capitals. The body and aisle have separate roofs, which are open, and of very plain timber. The beams rest on rude stone corbels. The east window is a large one of five lights, with very obtuse arch, following a pattern very common in this part. The other windows are small, and few in number, which makes the interior very dark. They are square-headed, of two or three lights. That at the east of the north aisle is Pointed, of three lights. The nave and aisle are about equal in width. The font has an octagonal bowl, set on a square base. Some of the original stalls remain, but out of their proper place, in the north aisle ; the poppy-heads have two wooden images, the front of the desks panelled. There is a curious old chest. The altar is much encroached upon by pews, and thrust out of its proper place. There is a deal box near it, for offerings at funerals.

Beddgelert (St. Mary).

August 1824, and July 1, 1864.

This church, though small, is loftier and of greater pretension than any others of the neighbourhood. It once belonged to a priory, and consists now of one undivided space of fair height, but on the north side are two very fine Early English arches in the wall, which once divided off a short aisle, now unhappily destroyed. These two arches have fine deep mouldings, unusual in Wales, and the pillars composed of clustered shafts, with moulded capitals. There are three orders of arch-mouldings, and the shafts are set at intervals, large and small. The east window is a fine triplet of considerable length and dignity, without shafts, but having mouldings. The west window is a small lancet. All other windows are modern insertions. The west doorway, within a modern porch, is very plain and Pointed. There is a rude west gallery, the pews tolerably uniform, and the walls covered with coffin-plates. The roof ceiled ; the font poor and doubtful. The west end is mantled with ivy, and over the gable is a bell-cot, with arch for one bell.

Bettws-y-Coed (St. Michael).

1825 and 1864.

Originally a very small church, with little or no architectural character; since enlarged and nearly

Effigy in Bettwys-y-Coed Church.
Scale, 1 inch to 1 foot.

rebuilt, and consisting now of a body and a kind of transept on the north, and a new bell-cot at the west end. The windows are very good modern Gothic. The roof is open, and seems to have some of the old timbers. The seats are all open. Under an arch in the wall, on the north of the chancel, is a slab, with effigy of a knight, having a lion at his feet, inscribed: "Hic jacet Grufyd ap Davyd Goch. Agnus Dei miserere mei."

CAERHUN (ST. MARY).

Sept. 1855.

This church has the usual undivided single body, with a large chapel on the south side, close to the east end: a Welsh feature. Over the west end is a bell-turret, of far more character than usual in Welsh churches, square at the top, but with a kind of small pediment, rising in the centre, and pierced by two arches for bells. The turret is set upon a horizontal corbel table, and on the space below the bell-arches is sculptured a small crucifix. The south porch has been restored. The windows are mostly bad on the south of the nave. The east window has three plain-Pointed lights, without tracery. In the south chapel are square-headed windows of three lights, of late character; that at its east end, of two lights, very wide, with foliated mullions. The font has a plain octagonal bowl. The seats are new and neat. There is a lych-gate; the churchyard is quiet and picturesque.

CARNARVON (ST. MARY'S CHAPEL).

May 8, 1873.

This is said to be the old garrison chapel, and is situated at the north-west corner of the old town walls, which bound it north and west, and one of the original round towers at the angle contains a bell. It has been much modernised, and it may be doubtful as to what parts are original. It consists now of a nave and short chancel, each with narrow north and south aisles. The nave has on each side four pointed arches, which look original, and have hoods and corbels. The pillars are of irregular octagonal form, and look as if they had been tampered with. The chancel is of one bay. The interior is fitted with pews and galleries, and has a good organ. The west wall has an odd Flamboyant window of four lights; the other windows are modern Gothic. The south side has buttresses and plain pinnacles.

CLYNOG (ST. BEUNO).

1824, 1839, 1848.

A late Third-Pointed cruciform church, on a scale far superior to the generality of Welsh churches, and not without reason considered the finest in North Wales, excepting perhaps Wrexham, Gresford, and Mold. There are no aisles: the nave and chancel are wide. There is a north porch, a sacristy, and a western tower; and adjacent to the church on the south-west, communicating with it by a covered passage from the steeple, is the chapel of St. Beuno, a later building than the church. The beauty of this church has been much exaggerated, fine as it is, for there is much of coarse and ordinary architecture, and the transepts are, as usual, awkwardly tacked on. The windows are large, and with four centred arches. Those on the north and south of the nave and chancel are of three lights. The east window is a very large one; those in the transept are of five lights. The tower is coarse and plain, probably very late, and has a battlement slightly tending to the saddle form. The belfry windows large, of three lights, and without foils on the north-east and west, but on the south merely a slit. It has a Tudor arch doorway, with label. The parapets of the church are embattled, and the nave has a tolerable wood roof, panelled, with bosses and pierced spandrels. The tower arch is Pointed, with plain mouldings. The crossing is clumsy, and wanting in effect. The transept is as at Holyhead, there being no north and south arches in the centre; but there are east and west ones opening to the chancel and nave; these are very wide and inelegant, springing from shafts. The transepts have very poor roofs. There is an ascent of three

Brass of William Glynne at Clynnog Fawr.

(*From a Rubbing by Mr. D. Griffith Davies.*)

steps about the middle of the nave. The rood-loft with its screen remains, of rather ordinary work, but having a semblance of being earlier than rood-loft screens usually are. The rood-turret and staircase is in the south transept; the staircase is extended also to the roof, and is lighted by slits looking into the chancel, one of which is a hagioscope, commanding the altar.

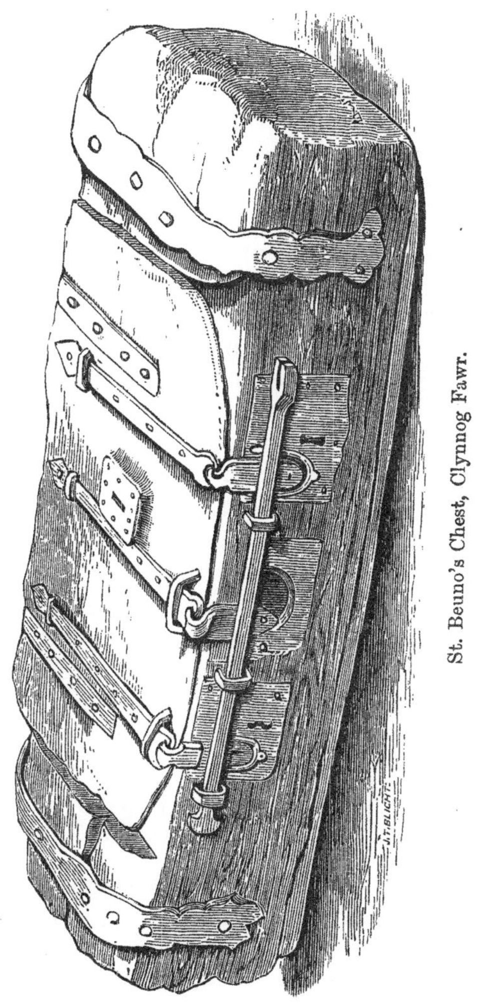

St. Beuno's Chest, Clynnog Fawr.

There is a south door, both to nave and chancel. The north porch is curious, of three stages, with steps from the exterior to the parvise. The outer door is lateral; the windows square-headed, of domestic character.

There is in the porch something resembling an aumbry, and very probably the upper storeys were used for the residence of a recluse. In the north transept is a square recess in the wall, near the ground. The chancel has returned stalls, with misereres and desks. In the wood-carving may be seen the eagle with two necks. Under the east window is a square aumbry. On the south side of the altar are three equal ogee-headed sedilias, crocketed and foliated with pinnacled octagonal piers, and also an octagonal piscina. The sacristy is gabled, and has a chamber over it. The lower part has incipient groining, and narrow square-headed windows. It has three aumbries, the eastern of which expands within the wall. There is an altar-tomb, A.D. 1667, to one of the Twisleton family, with rather a pretty chained border. Also, a small mural brass to William Glynne, a child, A.D. 1633. The font is a poor one, subsequent to the Restoration, with the date 1662.

The chapel of St. Beuno is inferior to the church; its battlement is destroyed, and there is much bare wall on the north and south. Its east window is of five lights, without foils, the west window, square-headed, of two lights; near the east end a small trefoiled piscina. The exterior is dirty, and out of order. Over the west door is a niche. There is a rude passage, connecting this chapel with the tower, which appears to be of comparatively modern date.

Conway (St. Mary).

1847.

This church is spacious and interesting, and, though with much of rough architecture, yet there is much of curious and superior work. The plan comprises a west tower, a nave with side aisles, south transept, and chancel. The whole is of a dark, coarse mountain stone. The tower has a plain battlement, and an unequal turret on its south side. On the west side a fair doorway, with shafts, above which are three unequal plain lancets. In the next stage, a two-light Decorated window; the belfry story is Perpendicular, with a square-headed window. There are north and south porches, the former rude; the latter has pleasing open wood roof, with feathering. Near both the north and south doors are very rude brackets internally. The nave has a plain ribbed roof, which is continued along the chancel, there being no chancel arch. The

Conway Church: Carved Capital of West Entrance to Tower.

windows of the side aisles are mostly square-headed and late, of three lights. The interior is striking, both from its length of uninterrupted roof and from the great beauty of the rood-loft screen, which remains in great perfection at the entrance to the chancel. There are also some very fine pieces of wood-carving amidst the pewing, some with pinnacles, open panelling, and armorial bearings. The nave is divided from each aisle by three lofty Pointed arches, with rather coarse mouldings, springing from octagonal plain columns, having overhanging capitals, and rather too large to fit the mouldings of the arches; a fourth arch on the

Sepulchral Slab of Dorothy Wynn in Conway Church.
Scale, $\frac{1}{18}$ actual size.
(*Drawn by Mr. D. Griffith Davies.*)

south side opens to the transept. Against the pier of the transept arch is a trefoiled niche, with arch moulding and dripstone. There is another feathered niche within the transept. The transept has a good

Decorated window of three lights, containing some ancient stained glass. The rood-loft screen is of great beauty, of five compartments, filled with excellent Perpendicular tracery; there is also fan-work groining, and rich cornices of vine leaf, etc. Upon the loft is set a small organ. There are two small square-headed windows, giving light to the rood-loft, and the door to it is in the transept. One window on the north side, opposite to the transept arch, and near the rood-loft, has three lancets within a general arch. The chancel has a Perpendicular east window; on the south a good early Decorated one of two lights; on the north a triple lancet, within a Pointed arch. On the north side of the chancel is the vestry, with two small windows, one Perpendicular, one Decorated. There are several fine ancient stalls, and desks before them, enriched with beautiful wood-carving, the ends especially fine. In the floor of the chancel is a slab, with the effigy ot a female in a square head-dress, and an inscription in Gothic letter, nearly illegible: this may be the foundress. There is a handsome chest, with date 1631. The font stands on steps in the proper position, in the centre of the west end of the nave. The font is a remarkably fine Perpendicular one, with beautiful quatrefoil panelling, upon a pedestal which has pierced panelling.

Criccieth (St. Catherine).

1839.

A small, neglected church in bad order, consisting of nave, north aisles and chancel, which are divided from each other by two very wide and flat arches, rather remarkable in form, having a plain rude pier (much altered since: the arcade now consists of a course of three odd-shaped and very flat arches on square plain piers). The roofs are plain and barnlike, but that part which is just over the altar is boarded in panels. The east window is Decorated, of two lights; in the east wall is a recess or locker, and a rude one on the south which may have been a piscina. Near the west door is a benatura. The east window of the north aisle is of three lights, within a Pointed arch, each trefoiled. The font is cylindrical and small, and there is a plain kneeling-bench attached to it. There is no steeple. Some pieces of stained glass yet remain.

DOLWYDELAN (S. GWYDDELAN).

October 3rd, 1850.

A Welsh church, much modernised and partly rebuilt at the expense of Lord Willoughby d'Eresby, in a creditable state of neatness. The church is short, and the chancel extends only a little eastward of the south transeptal chapel: that common Welsh appendage. There is a north porch, and the common single bell-gable over the west end. The roof is plain and open, but over the sacrarium has neat panelling with bosses. The chapel is debased, and opens to the church by two ugly obtuse arches, springing from a circular pillar, with square capital. Its windows are square-headed, with contracted arches. Another window on the south is a double lancet. There are crosses on the east gable and on the transept. There are several open benches, and the rood-screen is placed now near the west end of the nave, of plain and tolerable Third Pointed character: the spandrels of the door are foliated. The font is of doubtful kind: a sort of square trough, on a square stem. The pulpit and desk are on either side of the altar. There is an Elizabethan monument to one of the Wynnes of Gwydyr, and on the north of the chancel a small brass in a window-jamb.

EDERN (S. EDEYRN).

September 19th, 1847.

The church is plain and mean, having a chancel and and nave undistinguished, and a large awkward chapel on the north side of the former. Over the west end is an open-arched belfry. There are very few windows, and those mostly debased—none at all on the north side of the nave. The east window is square-headed, of three lights, debased. On the south side of the sacrarium is a narrow oblong one. The roof of each part is open, but varies—in the nave, very rude and plain ; that of the chancel has pierced quatrefoils above the collar with no very bad effect ; that in the transeptal chapel is somewhat similar and has some pretension to mouldings, and is full of pegs.[1] This chapel is joined to the chancel most clumsily, the timbers of the roof meeting those of the chancel most rudely—there seems to have been once an arch between them, now cut off. There is a poor and late screen across the nave, near the west end. The font is cylindrical, quite rude, on a square stem, much cracked and mutilated. There are some modern open benches, and a brick raised seat on the west side of the transept. The door is at the west end, the exterior very plain and scarcely church-like.

Gyffin.

August 21st, 1847.

A small, low church, yet somewhat longer and more interesting than most Welsh churches. It has a long nave, with narrow chancel, which has an aisle, or extension on the north, and a large chapel on the south reaching to the east end. Over the west end a small bell-gable. There are no windows north of the nave ; on the south are two square-headed ones without foils. On the south side of the chancel, and westward of its chapel, is a very curious doorway of First Pointed character, having very fair mouldings and three orders of shafts, with capitals of First Pointed foliage. This is unusual in North Wales. The nave is loftier than the chancel, and has a plain open roof of very rude timbers, but at its east end a covered boarded ceiling, divided

[1] *I.e.*, the roof timbers are fastened together with wooden pegs.

into panels by ribs with bosses, and curiously painted with figures of saints of large size. The construction of the roof is very clumsy. On the north side of the chancel are two wooden columns supporting the roof. Between the chancel and south chapel is a wood screen of Third Pointed character, above which is a board inscribed in Black Letter with texts in Welsh. There is some trace of fresco painting on the north wall of this chapel. Its windows are square-headed, Third Pointed, of three lights, simply trefoiled. The east windows of the chancel, and of the south chapel, are of similar character. On the north of the chancel are some ugly modern windows. There is a wooden south porch; and on the south side, near the west end, one window is merely a plain slit.

Llanaelhaiarn (St. Aelhaiarn).

September 13th, 1848.

A small cruciform church, low as usual, with ill-developed transepts, and a bell-gable over the west end. The roof is open in the nave, but in the chancel, which is not equal to the nave in height, it is boarded. The transepts have been awkwardly tacked on, according to the Welsh fashion: not opening originally by arches, but merely wooden piers, and extending very near to the east end. Some improvements have lately been effected in the church, and two other arches added between the transepts and the chancel. The east window has three obtuse-headed equal lights; the other windows are late and poor. The rood-screen is Late, has in the centre a flat arch forming the door, and three compartments of pierced panelling on each side. Near one of the doors is a small benatura. There is very little architectural character about the church. The old font was a cylindrical one, broken; a new one of octagonal form, much too small, is now in use. There are open benches in the chancel and transepts.

LLANBEBLIC (ST. PEBLIC).

September 14, 1848.

A larger church than is usually found in North

Sepulchral Effigy in Llanbeblig Church.

Wales, but with few interesting architectural features, and much modernised. The plan is cruciform, with the usual clumsy transepts and a western tower. The nave has no aisles, but there is an aisle or chapel on the north of the chancel. There is a north porch. The external walls are whitewashed. The tower, which has very thick walls, is rude and without buttresses, having a graduated battlement. On the west side a low door, on the south a plain slit; the belfry window on each side square-headed. The arch between the tower and nave is a plain-Pointed one, somewhat altered. There are some square-headed late

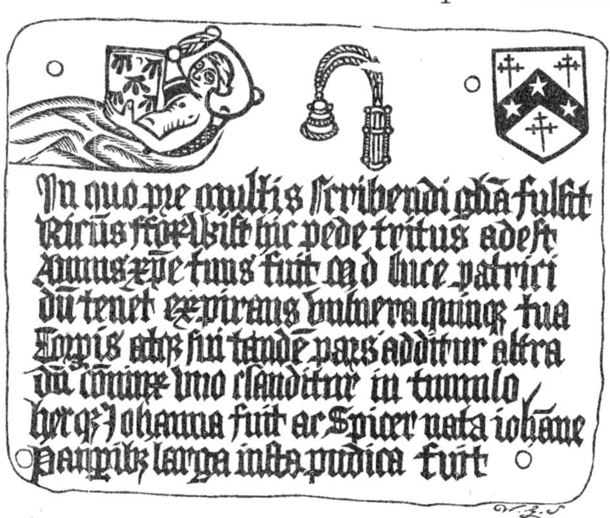

Sepulchral Brass in South Wall of Chancel of Llanbeblig Church. Scale, ⅓ natural size.

windows in the nave, and some poor modern ones. In the south transept is a Third-Pointed one of five lights. The chancel has an east window of four lights, and one on the south of three, also Third Pointed, and one Middle Pointed one on the south, of two lights. The north chapel is gabled, and has a Middle-Pointed window of two lights, having an acute arch and a double-feathered trefoil in the head. At the east end of the same is a four-light window of debased work, without foils. The chancel is embattled, the rest of the church has a slate roof. Near the north door is a benatura. The interior is frightfully spoiled and encumbered. A huge and very deep gallery occupies nearly all the nave; and the pulpit, though not in the centre, has its back to the altar. The roof has arched timbers, and an embattled cornice. The transepts do not open by arches; the chancel arch is modern. The north chapel opens to the chancel by a Tudor-shaped arch, with octagonal piers. In this chapel is a late but rich alabaster tomb, with panelled sides and recumbent effigies, with Italian ornamental features, to Sir Wm. Gryffyth, Knt., A.D. 1593. At the end of the south transept is an ogee sepulchral recess, with crockets and bold feathering, and still retaining traces of colour. The font has an octagonal bowl, very plain.

LLANBEDR (ST. PETER).

May 28, 1858.

This genuine Welsh church is in neat condition. The plan is a nave and chancel, with a kind of transept or chapel on the south side of the latter. A south porch, and a little open bell-cot over the west gable. The roof is open, the windows mostly late and square-headed, of two lights; but the western of three, and the eastern, is a poor modern imitation of Norman. There is no chancel arch; but the south chapel is divided from the chancel by two very obtuse and debased arches, with octagonal piers, having a plain capital. The font has a small circular bowl, set on a modern stem. The porch doorway is rude and obtuse. The situation pretty, on an eminence looking over the vale of Conway.

LLANBEDROG.

July 30, 1852.

A long, narrow church, with the usual open belfry, situated in a beautiful churchyard, shaded with fine trees, and presenting a most picturesque appearance. The windows are modern and bad. There is a plain rood-screen of Perpendicular character, and a very ordinary octagonal font.

Llanberis (St. Peris).

August 31, 1853.

A small cruciform church, with low walls, sprawling transepts unsatisfactorily attached, and a bell-gable at the west end. The walls seem to have been wholly rebuilt, and the interior neatly restored, but so as to keep up the original character. The roof is open, with good rude timber-work, and over the sacrarium is a panelled boarded ceiling. They are no arcades, but plain stone piers supporting the roof. The windows are newly inserted, and Perpendicular ; the font new; the seats mostly open.

Llandegai.

September 5, 1858.

This church is somewhat interesting, being a complete cruciform church, with central tower : an unusual form in Wales. It is small and has no aisles ; but the general character is pleasing, though without fine details. Of late years it has undergone a complete renovation, and is extremely neat and in creditable condition, though the new work is open to criticism. The churchyard, too, is very beautiful, and the village generally a pattern of neatness and good order. The prevailing character is late Perpendicular, as usual. The tower is not square, but smaller from east to west, so that the four large pointed arches beneath it are not similar in size. They spring from circular shafts, with capitals. The chancel is very short, and the sacrarium laid with encaustic tiles. The windows are renewed on the south ; the others of the rude Welsh type, without foils or tracery, of three lights, except the eastern, which has five. There is no west window, but a modern low porch, which is the chief entrance. The nave is fitted with open seats, and there is a nice finger organ in the west gallery. In the chancel is a rich alabaster tomb of the Renaissance work of the

14[2]

sixteenth century; also a plain mural monument to the celebrated Archbishop Williams, *obt.* 1650. The walls have embattled parapets.

Llandudno, Old Church (St. Tudno).

June 22, 1852.

This deserted and dilapidated church presents now a melancholy spectacle, in an elevated and lonely spot not far from the Great Orme's Head. It is all in one space, without aisles or distinction of chancel; with very low walls, and a small bell-gable for one bell at the west end. The windows are very few: only one on the north, which is single and obtuse-headed, but probably late, and one on the south, which is of two lights, labelled and square-headed, of late character; the east window of three lights, trefoliated and Perpendicular. There is no west window, but a plain west door, and a plain north door, with porch. The roof is of a common type, and open; that in the eastern part is more worked, having mouldings and an embattled cornice. In the east wall is a Pointed piscina, with shelf, and in the sacrarium two curious gravestones, with finely-sculptured crosses of excellent pattern, but unhappily cracked.

NOTES ON THE OLDER CHURCHES

IN THE

FOUR WELSH DIOCESES.

BY THE LATE SIR STEPHEN R. GLYNNE, BART.

(*Continued from* p. 188.)

LLANARMON (ST. GERMAN).

June 20th, 1861.

THE church, rather large for this part of the country, consists of two equal aisles or bodies—no unfrequent arrangement in North Wales—and is wholly of plain Perpendicular character. There is neither steeple nor porch, only a bell-cot over the west end, for one bell, in an open arch. There is a break in the arcade marking the division of the chancel, but none in the roof, and the chancel portion is about equal in length to the nave. There are two wide flat arches in each, of late date, upon octagonal columns and clustered octagonal shafts, attached to the pier which forms the break, whence spring the arches. The two east windows are of three lights, that ending the southern aisle the best, the other having a transom. The other windows are very poor, of two and three lights, but many have been mutilated. The roof is of the open Welsh kind, with quatrefoil piercing in the timbers, all very rude. The condition of the church is miserable: the walls and floor damp, and the windows with broken glass.

LLANDUDWEN IN LLEYN (ST. TUDWEN).

May 28th, 1873.

This small church is obscurely situated and not easily found, and, withal but a mean structure of the local type. It has a nave with north and south transepts set on at the east, and no regular chancel. The walls are very low, and there is only one window in the nave, which is debased, on the south side. The transepts have square-headed windows of three lights, debased and unfoliated. The roof is of open timbers. Over the west end is a bell-cot for one bell, in an open arch.

LLANEUGAN (ST. EINION, FRENHIN).

July 31st, 1852.

A large church, comprising a nave and chancel, each with south aisle, a west tower and south porch, the whole late Perpendicular. There is no architectural distinction between the nave and chancel, but there are fine screens, with lofts extending across both the chancel and south aisle, which forms the remarkable feature in this church. The arcade of the nave is of four Tudor-shaped arches, the piers moulded with capitals. In the chancel there are two coarse arches of dissimilar character—one Pointed and wide, one obtuse and narrow, and both without mouldings, with plain pier, having no capital. The windows are mostly square-headed and of three lights, that at the east of the south aisle Pointed. The roofs are Welsh, with the usual quatrefoils. The screens are very elegant, and panelled; that to the chancel has two vine-leaf cornices. The screen to the south aisle has the loft remaining, with panelling below it, and the same cornices. The roof of the chancel is inferior to that of the nave; there are some stalls in the chancel with poppy-heads; in the east wall is a stone bracket; over the sacrarium the roof is, as usual, boarded and panneled; the tower arch is Pointed and continuous; the tower is embattled, and has small pinnacles; the belfry windows are of two lights; there is no west door; the west window partially built up; the staircase partially displaces the south belfry window. The porch is large, but without parvise; the outer door of

Tudor form, with octagonal shafts ; the inner has continuous mouldings. The font is octagonal and small, with quatrefoils and roses, late and poor. The church is pewed, and, on the whole, neat.

Llanfair Fechan (St. Mary).

August 21st, 1847.

A very rude cruciform church, with large transepts clumsily put together, and no arches at the crossing. At the west end, a Welsh bell-gable. In the north transept is one narrow slit for a window, with internal splay, and on the east side of the southern transept one somewhat similar. There is a trace of a lychnoscope on the south-west of the chancel, set obliquely, and near it appear to have been steps. The east window is square-headed, Third Pointed, of three lights. There are upright wooden posts of rude character forming the divisions of the transepts ; the benches are open, but modern. The windows beyond those mentioned are bad modern insertions. The font has an octagonal bowl alternately panelled with quatrefoils, bearing the date 1665, and inscribed "*ex dono Grifini Rectoris,*" 1848. Llanfair Fechan Church is condemned to be pulled down and rebuilt. The new church consecrated, October 11th, 1849.

Llanfair Isgaer (St. Mary).

August 20th, 1855.

This church has a remarkable site, away from houses, on an eminence close to the Menai. It consists of a nave and chancel undivided, with an open belfry over the west end. The chancel is clearly developed. There are no windows on the north, and the few that are on the south are closed by shutters. The east window of ordinary character.

Llanfihangel, Bachellaeth-in-Lleyn (St. Michael).

May 28th, 1873.

It is uncertain whether any part of this church is original, but there are indications that the substructure of the walls may be so. There is, however, no architectural character in the church, except the old font, which has an octagonal bowl diminishing downwards, but much mutilated. The church is a plain oblong, with raised walls and modern Gothic windows; in a dreary situation, but in decent order.

Llangelynin (by Conway) St. Celynin.

1862.

This, the original parish church, is now forsaken and dilapidated, on account of its very remote and insulated situation; a new church having been built in a more populous part of the parish. The site of the old church is peculiarly lonely and inaccessible; on an elevated spot amongst the hills, out of sight of all habitations. It is of the Welsh type, of no very uncommon form; a nave and chancel all in one space, with a large transverse chapel clumsily added on to the north of the chancel, and ranging very nearly with its east end. There is a south porch, and over the west end a small bell-gable for one bell. The walls are low. The porch has a wood gable and stone benches; near the door is a stoup. There is no chancel arch, but the base of the rood-screen remains; the roof is of rude timber, and barnlike, but in the eastern part of cradle form and ribbed. The east window is Perpendicular, of plain character, square-headed, and labelled of three lights. In the east wall internally is some puzzling work, consisting of unfinished panelling, with trefoiled arches of no very different character from the window, yet looking as if an original design had been interrupted and supplanted. The transeptal chapel opens by no arch, but merely has rude posts of wood supporting a horizontal beam: its floor is raised, and it appears to have been used for burials; its east window is a sort of lancet, but of doubtful age. There are no windows whatever on the north side. The font has a plain octagonal bowl, upon a short, rude stem. Nothing can exceed the wretchedness of this church; externally, the roof is much out of repair, and the slates kept on chiefly by large stones placed upon them: within, the arrangement was always miserable, with a small, confined sacrarium and altar, flanked by pulpit and reading-pew. The pews are rotting. One south window is of three lights, unfoliated, merely with a mullion, square-headed.

Llangian.

July 30th, 1852.

This church has been in great measure rebuilt, and has a completely modern appearance. The windows are quasi-lancets, inserted; and a west door has been added in the same style. The form is the common one, without aisles. The original Welsh roof seems to have been untouched.

Llangwnadl (St. Gwynodl).

September 4th, 1855.

This church, though small, is remarkable for having the triple division, *i.e.*, a body with north and south aisles, very unusual in North Wales. There is, however, no distinction of chancel, and the church being very short, and wide at the same time, has the appearance of being almost square. The whole is Perpendicular. The arcades are each of three arches, wide and low, and of Tudor form; the piers are octagonal, those on the south having capitals, but not those on the north. There are three east windows, of three lights, and rather ordinary Perpendicular tracery. The other windows also are late; some square-headed, some Pointed. The church is in good condition, and very neat within, having been repaired and restored in 1850. The seats are all open, and there is a new pulpit and desk. The belfry is also new, over the west gable, containing one bell. The font has an octagonal bowl with sculpture on the sides, representing heads.

Llangybi (St. Cybi).

January 20, 1861.

This church has only a nave and chancel, undivided, having a plain bell-gable over the west end. All the windows have been mutilated except the eastern one, Perpendicular, and of three lights; the others, square-headed and labelled. The roof is open in the nave, but boarded over the sacrarium. There is a rude recess in the north wall of the chancel. The font has a plain octagonal bowl, set on a square. The site is pretty, but there is no one feature of interest.

Llaniestyn (St. Jestyn).

September 4th, 1855.

This church has an undivided body with south aisle, and open belfry over the west end. The aisle does not extend quite to the west end, but is divided from the body by five Tudor arches, of low proportions, springing from very low octagonal piers with capitals. The whole is of late date. The windows are all modernised. The font has an octagonal bowl, with rather coarse tracery and figures.

Llanllyfni (St. Rhedyw).

July 16, 1850.

A rude cruciform church of the Welsh type, with awkward transepts, set very close to the east end; a south porch and a small open belfry at the west end. The roof of the nave and transepts is of the Welsh open kind, with rude foliations. That of the chancel is boarded, having a roughish cornice. There are no arches to the transepts or chancel, but upright shafts of wood. The east window and one in the south transept are Third Pointed, of three lights, merely trifoliated. Others are square-headed, some foliated and some not. Between the nave and chancel is a modern loft, occupying the place of the ancient rood-loft, and on each side of it a rude stone pier, both of which are perforated. That on the north has an oblong recess and niche. There are also the original rude stone steps. The fittings are extremely rude and homely, and some plain open seats. The altar is set at right-angles with the wall, within a ludicrously small sacrarium, enclosed by rails, and not in the centre of it. The font is a plain octagonal bowl. Set against the north wall, near the door, and not far from it, is what seems to have been a benatura. The north and south doors are Pointed.

Llannor (Holy Cross).

September 18th, 1849.

A long narrow church without aisles, but having the chapel tacked on to the south of the chancel. At the west end is a slender tower of saddle-back form, the gables being graduated rudely. It has no buttresses, and the belfry window is a plain oblong slit. The roof is open, and a good Welsh specimen. There is only one north window and that is near the east end, and the aisle itself is a modern one. Those on the south of the nave are also very poor, but the east window is a tolerable First Pointed triplet, without mouldings. The south chapel opens to the chancel by a very plain low arch, with continuous orders. This chapel is large and projects like a transept; has a west door, and square-headed debased windows without foils. There are some open seats and some pews.

Llanrhychwyn.

July 1st, 1856.

This small church is on a very secluded site, and is approached through the woods which clothe the steep side of the hill behind Gwydir and Trefriw. There is, near to it, a good view of Carnedd Llewelyn and other mountains. It consists of two short equal bodies, and has a bell-niche over the west end. The division between the two bodies is formed by four rude square stone pillars, supporting a horizontal entablature or cornice, without arches. The walls are thick and rude. The altar occupies the end of the southern aisle; the east window is square-headed, of two lights, and contains some stained glass. The other east window is modernised. Some other windows are modern, others square-headed, of one and two lights, one without foils. The font is a plain cylindrical bowl on a step. The pulpit bears the date 1691. The seats are open and new. There is a lych-gate to the churchyard.

Llanrug.

June 25th, 1858.

A quasi-cruciform church without aisles, having the little Welsh bell-cot and north porch.

Llanwnda (St. Gwyndav).

A small, rude, cruciform church, with a turret containing two bells. The transepts have square-headed Perpendicular windows, one of good character, with label and corbel heads. There is a large excrescence on the north side, used as a school, and a rude wooden porch. The east window has three other lancets, but it is not clear whether they are original. There are rude pointed arches opening from the nave to the transepts, but no division of chancel. Above the east end of the chancel the roof is boarded. The interior is very gloomy, and the fittings of the rudest kind. Near one of the doors is an octagonal benatura. There is a bracket for a niche in the north transept, and a rude niche on the south of the altar. The font is a rude octagonal mass. The north transept contains monuments to the Bulkeleys. Rebuilt entirely.

Penmachno (St. Tyddud).

October 3rd, 1850.

This church is in an extremely bad state of dilapidation. The plan is a common one: a nave and chancel, with no architectural distinction, and a large chapel on the south side of the latter. Over the west end, an arched gable for one bell. There are very few windows, and the walls are very low. There is a plain north porch. The east window is Third Pointed, of three lights, simply trefoiled. The chapel opens to the chancel by an ugly misshapen arch springing from imposts. At the east end of this chapel is a plain window without tracery, and a door. The roof is of a common character, and not a bad specimen, the timbers being rudely foliated. Over the sacrarium is the usual boarded, panelled ceiling. The principal feature in the church is the rood-screen, which is a fair Third-Pointed specimen, though much mutilated. Its compartments have tracery in the heads. The font is a rude cylinder, on a square base. In the east window is a little stained glass; and in the jamb of it is an ancient painting on wood, representing a French saint, a friar, and an executioner. Nothing can exceed the rudeness of the open benches; but there are some odd pews: one enclosed with a kind of railing, another having at the angles carved posts with coarsely-executed heads. The altar is, as usual, shoved out of its place by the pulpit and pews. There is an old west gallery, and a very rough pavement. The church-yard is very large.

Pistyll.

July 17th, 1850.

A small church, situated in a lonely spot, on an eminence looking over Carnarvon Bay. It has no aisles nor distinction of chancel, but all in one space; and has the usual arched gable, with one bell, at the west end. There are no windows in the north side, except a slit near the east end. Those on the south are modern Gothic, and the eastern one a bad square one. The only entrance is at the west end. The interior is primitive, the roof open and rude. On the south-east side is a square recess in the wall. The font is curious: cylindrical in form, swelling towards the base, and set on a square. It is sculptured with rude scroll-work, knobs, etc., apparently of an early character. The seats are chiefly open.

Rhiew (St. Aelrhyw).

September 7th, 1858.

A small, rude church, of the clumsy quasi-cruciform plan, with small bell-cot. The architectural features are poor. The roof is open; the windows modern and without character, except one narrow slit in the south transept, and there are no arches within, and the walls low; but the situation lofty, and commanding a fine view.

Trefriew (St. Mary).

August 21st, 1847.

A small church, consisting of two short and equal aisles, without distinction of chancel, and an ivied belfry over the west end. The interior has a very rough and primitive character; and nothing can exceed the rudeness of the arches, if they can be so called, opening between the aisles. They are very flat and ill-shaped, and between them a solid square pier of masonry. There is a stoup near the south door. The benches all open, and exceedingly plain.

NOTES ON THE OLDER CHURCHES

IN THE

FOUR WELSH DIOCESES.

BY THE LATE SIR STEPHEN R. GLYNNE, BART.

(*Continued from* p. 188, vol. xvii.)

DIOCESE OF BANGOR.

MERIONETH.

LLANABER, ST. BODVAN (ST. MARY).

1841.

A LARGER and better church than usual in this part, the work being for the most part of genuine and elegant Early English character. The plan consists of a nave, with high clerestory and low aisles, a south porch and a chancel. Over the south porch rises a turret containing a bell. Within the south porch is a beautiful Early English doorway, equal to the best work in that style that is found in England, but perhaps verging to Decorated. There are five or six courses of arch mouldings, the shafts—three on each side—bearing fine capitals of oak foliage. The church is, unhappily, very much out of repair, damp, and altogether neglected, and from its situation very much exposed to the violence of the elements. The roofs are tiled and the aisles low; the nave is divided from each by five low Pointed arches, springing from circular pillars, some of which have octagonal capitals with foliage. The western arch on the north is closed, and a lumber place formed. The chancel arch has good mouldings, springing from shafts, with capitals bearing foliage of somewhat Norman character. There is an ascent of one step into the chancel. The clerestory of the nave is high, and genuine Early English, with single lancets. At the east end of the south aisle there appears to have been an altar. The chancel has a single lancet at the east end with mouldings ; on the south a much plainer one, and on the north a Late square-headed window. The roof of the chancel is open to the timbers, with quatrefoils rudely carved in the compartments. A large chapel, of more modern date, is added to the north side of the chancel. There is part of a wooden screen, with pierced panelling, and remnants of the stalls and desks before them. There are lancets closed at the east end of the aisles. The font is an octagonal bowl, panelled with quatrefoils, upon a circular stem. Coffin-plates, as usual, cover the walls. The west gable is finished by a small turret.

Llanbedr (St. Peter).

September 1, 1852.

This church has a nave and properly distinguished chancel, with the usual little Welsh open belfry over the west end. Contrary to North Wales custom there is a chancel arch, but coarse and ill-shaped, and without mouldings. There are no windows on the north or at the west end. The east window is of two lights, mutilated, and on the south of the altar is a single rude light. In the east wall is a small recess. There is an indication of a low rude arch in the north wall of the chancel, whence it seems likely that there was once an aisle or chapel adjoining. The roof is of the common type, but rather superior in the chancel, and there is a longitudinal rib in the centre, and a cornice which has a kind of chequered work. The font has a plain octagonal bowl on a stem raised on steps. The church is partially new pewed. Over the altar is a piece of boarded ceiling in panels.

Llandanwg (St. Tanwg).

August 31, 1852.

This church is now forsaken, and falling fast to ruin, an ugly new church having been built at Harlech. Its situation is lonely, close to the sea shore; the form much like Llanfair, without architectural distinction of chancel. Over the west end is the usual small open belfry. There is a plain west door, but no windows. The roof is open, and a fair specimen of its kind, with quatrefoils, and above the altar sixfoil rude sculpture. The east window is Perpendicular, of three lights, partially closed; on the north and south of the sacrarium are coarse windows of two trefoiled lights, with cill prolonged. Over the sacrarium is a boarded ceiling, painted and panelled, on which are represented figures of saints, and of the four evangelists. The interior presents a wretched appearance of dilapidated and decaying pews.

Llanddwywe (St. Ddwywe).

September 20, 1855.

This church has a nave and chancel, with the large transeptal chapel on the north of the chancel, so common in Wales. Over the west end a new bell-turret, erected 1853. The church is neat, and some improvements are being carried out. The roof has bold, rude foliation above the collar, but the ceiling of the chancel is plastered. The windows, as usual, are all Late, some with plain trefoiled heads. The east window of three lights; on the east side of the chapel are two single windows. Some stained glass has lately been inserted. There is no chancel arch, nor any to the north chapel, the division of which is formed by a large wood screen of open character, and rather Late and plain. This chapel has monuments of the family of Corsygedol. Many of the seats are open. The font has a plain octagonal bowl. The porch has the date 1593.

10 [2]

Llanegryn (St. Egryn).

August 31, 1850.

A small church, without aisles or architectural distinction of chancel, having a western bell-turret and south porch. It has lately been greatly improved by the munificence of W. W. E. Wynne, Esq., and contrasts favourably with the neglected condition of its neighbours, and further restoration and improvement is intended. The great and remarkable feature of Llanegryn is the elaborate rood-loft, which is in a perfect state, and lately put into good repair by judicious restoration. It is almost too large for the church, and reaches nearly to the roof. The work is Third Pointed; the loft has two fine vine-leaf cornices, and a Tudor flower one above. In the upper part are small buttresses, forming subdivisions, each crowned by a kind of little pedestal, possibly to support images. The east front is richer than the western, and has a range of pierced panelling presenting varied patterns. In the centre is a wide feathered arch for the door; on each side three smaller obtuse-arched compartments, also feathered. The roof is an open Welsh one, with spandrels and trefoiled spaces above the collar. Over the sacrarium is the boarded ceiling, painted and enriched lately with ribs and bosses. The windows are all recent insertions, in place of former barbarous ones. The east window, of three lights, Middle Pointed, copied from that of Llandysilio in Anglesey. On the south side are some of two lights, with square heads, of Third Pointed work. That at the west, transition from First to Middle Pointed, of two lights, with circle above. There are no north windows, except a Late square-headed one in the chancel. There is an ascent of two steps at the west end, rather unusual. The gallery has disappeared, and a new arrangement of the seats is contemplated. The altar is elegantly vested, and the sacrarium laid with encaustic tiles. The font is Norman, in shape of a cushioned capital reversed, and set on a cylindrical stem, with square plinth. The porch is plain, with roof like the nave; the bell-turret quite new and elegant, having a pointed gable and a flattened trefoil-opening, with one bell. In the south wall is a stone, inscribed with an ancient cross. There is a lych-gate near the east end of the church, and the churchyard occupies almost entirely the north side of the church, and only a small space on the south side, where the ground falls rapidly.

Llanelltyd (St. Illtyd).

June 16, 1867.

A small single church without distinction of chancel, with low walls, and at the west end a Pointed stone bell-cot for one bell, carried on stone corbels, which appears ancient. The roof may probably be original, with the old timbers arranged in Welsh fashion. Possibly the walls may be old, but all the windows are modern: the interior presents no remarkable feature.

Llanfair (St. Mary).

August 31, 1852.

A long, narrow church of a common type, with low walls and undistinguished chancel, and traces of a north aisle or chapel, now destroyed; but some plain obtuse arches are visible in the wall of the chancel. Here is the usual small open belfry at the west end. The chancel seems to occupy nearly half the length of the church; the roof is open. The east window is Perpendicular, of three lights. On the south-east is a small plain single window with stepped sill; and there is a Late and poor rood-screen. There is no west door nor window. In the north wall, near the west end of the nave, is an octagonal stoup. The font has an octagonal bowl, quite plain. There are ugly pews, and the walls are decorated by coffin-plates.

Llanfihangel y Pennant (St. Michael).

September 2, 1850.

A poor church, having the single undivided body with a clumsy transeptal chapel on the north, a south porch, and over the west end a bell-gable. There are scarcely any features which can be called architectural. The east window appears debased, but may have been altered, of three lights, with transom ; and one at the east end of the transept has two obtuse lights ; the others are modern. The roof is of timber, rather inferior to the ordinary Welsh roof, and has tie-beams. The transept, as usual, is clumsily tacked on and too large in proportion ; it opens by no arch, and its timbers are awkwardly joined to those of the nave. Over the sacrarium is the common boarded ceiling. The altar is very poor, and the pews encroach upon it. The walls are very low. The supports of the west gallery seem to be formed by parts of the late rood-loft screen, which is of somewhat debased character. The font is a good Norman one, the bowl square and scalloped on its lower edge ; the stem cylindrical, on a high square base ; it is lined with lead. The porch is plain and without character. There is a lych-gate.

Llanfihangel y Traethau (St. Michael).

August 17, 1861.

Mean and small and much modernised, but possibly the walls may be original. The plan is nearly oblong, without aisles, and no distinction of chancel ; a western porch, and open bell-cot for one bell. The west doorway has a plain Pointed arch. All the windows are modern, and the roof seems to have been renewed. The interior is paved quite up to the altar. The font has a plain octagonal bowl on a stem. In the churchyard is an ancient inscribed stone, on which the characters are difficult to decipher. The churchyard is lonely and elevated, commanding a fine view.

Llangelynin (St. Celynin).

August 31, 1850.

The old parish church, now deserted and used only for burials, stands in a lonely situation hanging over the sea; an ugly new one having been built in a more populous part of the parish. It has a single undivided space forming nave and chancel, and a large south porch, over which is a bell-gable for one bell, which bears the date 1660. At the west end is a narrow lancet-like window, much splayed, but square at the top, which seems to be First Pointed, opening internally by an obtuse arch. There are scarcely any windows on the north; one at the north-east is modern, as is that at the east, and some on the south. At the south-east is a Third Pointed one, with square head of two lights. The roof is rather low-pitched, but presents no very bad appearance: there are tie-beams, with spandrels and small shafts and upright timbers between the tie-beams and the slope of the roof. There is some trace of a debased rood-screen, the lower part being rather poor pierced panelling. Over the sacrarium there is the usual coved ceiling. On the north and south of the sacrarium are wide and flat arched recesses in the wall, but not quite similar in size; that on the north comes down lowest, and has a ledge on its east side. On the north side, westward of the other, is an oblong aperture in the wall, of small size. The interior is in a miserable state of neglect. There is a west gallery, and some mean open benches with some pews. On the north side is the mark of a small arched aperture in the wall, now closed, which may be of lychnoscopic nature. The font is poor and apparently debased, the bowl octagonal, with no drain and a square base. The porch is very plain, and contains a stoup; the inner door is remarkably low, both doors Pointed. The ground is uneven, ascending eastward. The view over the boundless sea, with the extensive line of coast from Lleyn to Pembrokeshire, is very striking.

Mallwyd (St. Tydecho).

This small church has scarcely any architectural features, and consists of a mean western steeple and a body without aisles. The east window has a depressed arch and transom, probably about the age of Elizabeth. The other windows are wretchedly mean. The steeple is of wood, slated, and bears this inscription: SOLI DEO SACRVM A° XTI MDCXI. The interior resembles a barn, but the eastern portion has an arched wood ceiling, with beams or brackets with rude heads. The pews are irregularly placed and very ugly, bearing the dates 1650 and 1716. The chief singularity is the position of the altar, in the centre of the church, surrounded by mean rails. The altar has a black marble slab, given in 1734 by John Mytton. The font is small, of octagonal form, of black marble. From the churchyard is a fine view, and in it is a large yew tree, fifteen yards round. In the churchyard is a monument to three twins (*sic*) Susannah, Catherine, and Ann Howels, who died at the of 11, 31 and 31.

Talyllyn (St. Mary).

September 2, 1850.

The form resembles that of Llanfihangel y Pennant, except that the transeptal chapel here is set on the south side. The bell-turret is more finished, being constructed of good stone with better masonry, which is carried down the whole of the west front in a continued line with it. The rest of the walls are of the usual coarse, slaty stone. The door is Pointed, the windows all debased; one in the transept of two lights, as at Llanfihangel; another of three square lights without foils. The roof is of tolerable pitch, and of the accustomed Welsh formation of timbers. Over the sacrarium a boarded ceiling. The font is Norman. The site is beautiful, looking over the lake, and bounded by Cader Idris.

Towyn (St. Cadvan).

August, 1839.

This is a cruciform church, large and more interesting in its architecture than usual. The whole is built of dark slaty stones, and the tower at the west end is low, modern, and plain. The nave is divided from each aisle by three very rude semicircular arches, on low round pillars, of Norman character. The clerestory windows are Norman, but all closed internally. The transepts open to the aisles by smaller arches than those in the nave, very low and small, but of like form. The chancel is without aisles, and opens to the nave by a plain-Pointed arch. Its east window is Perpendicular, of three lights ; the others are mostly mutilated or modern. The roof is open, but barn-like. There are crowded pews and a gallery over the eastern portion of the nave, but the western extremity is cut off, and free from pews. There are two monumental remains in the chancel, within Pointed arches in the wall ; one is the effigy of a knight in chain armour, and the arch has a fine crocketed ogee canopy. The altar is thrown out of its proper place by vile pews. The font is an octagonal basin, on a pedestal of like form.

Trawsfynnyd (St. Madryn).

June 17, 1867.

This church has been lately restored, and the interior put into very decorous condition. It consists of two long, low, parallel aisles, the chancel occupying the east end of the northern. The walls are probably original, and the masonry at the west end is of rude, large stones. There is also a south porch, and over the west gable of the nave a small bell-cot. The windows are all new insertions ; mostly square-headed, of two lights, and Perpendicular. Some pieces of coloured glass are preserved. The original arcade has been destroyed, and the two aisles are now divided by wooden pillars, or rather posts, supporting a horizontal cornice. The roofs seem original, of the Welsh kind, with open timbers and arched beams in some parts, with pierced quatrefoil in the point. The new seats are low and uniform, but have doors, and the wood-work is mostly varnished. There are no west windows. The font is octagonal, and cased in carved woodwork.

MONTGOMERYSHIRE.

Cemmaes (St. Tydecho).

September 9, 1856.

This church has a single nave and chancel, and is wider than its neighbour (Penegoes). A south porch and a slated belfry at the west end. The chancel is undivided, but marked by a difference in the roof, and is nearly equal in length to the nave. The chancel roof is coved, with ribs and bosses. On the north and south of the chancel are slit-like windows, like that at Penegoes, but much splayed and set rather obliquely. That on the north is closed. The east window, a plain one of two lights, apparently Perpendicular; the other windows bad. There is a carved Jacobean pew on the north side, and a monument of fair work, though unecclesiastical, to Sir Roger Mostyn, A.D. 1744. The seats are partly open. Under the west gallery is part of the rood-screen, with a good horizontal cornice of vine leaves intermixed with figures. The font is small, and partly of wood. There is a lych-gate, and the churchyard is very spacious.

Llanbrynmair (St. Mary).

September 17, 1863.

A neat church, partly rebuilt of late years, and presenting few features that seem to be original. It has a wide nave and chancel undivided, and a large transeptal chapel on the north, awkwardly tacked on. Over the west end is a Pointed belfry of wood, containing three bells, supported by strong timbers set on the ground. The windows are square-headed, of two and three lights, and seem to have been renewed; the east window rather poor; some windows have new stained glass. The transept is separated from the body by a huge octagonal pillar of oak, which supports a heavy beam and framework borne on spandrels: a clumsy arrangement without an arch. The roofs are open, with tie-beams; the seats are all open and new, and the condition of the church very creditable. The chancel, though confined, is stalled, and there is an organ in the transept, behind which is formed a vestry. There is an obtuse-headed recess south of the altar, probably for a piscina; and a still ruder one facing it on the north. The pulpit has some Late wood-carving. The font has a plain circular bowl on an octagonal stem.

Llandinam (St. Llonio).

October 30, 1855.

This church has a beautiful situation on a steep eminence looking over the vale of the Severn. It has been barbarously mutilated and altered,[1] especially within. The original roof is replaced by a wretched ceiling of plaster. The nave seems to have had originally only a south aisle, but the former arcade has been removed, and there are now two ranges of ugly columns, which causes a most awkward and unsightly irregularity, and destroys the proper arrangement. The chancel roof is lower than that of the nave. The windows are Perpendicular on the north, square-headed, of three lights; the others Pointed, of three lights. In the north wall of the chancel are two sepulchral recesses with moulded arches; and in the north-east angle a stone bracket upon a corbel-head. The

[1] The alteration took place about 1808.

tower arch has good mouldings ; the tower has an odd door on the south side with imposts, and is surmounted by the wooden pointed cage so common in this neighbourhood. Attached to the south side of the tower is a wooden porch, and the west side is strengthened by a large buttress. The unevenness of the ground causes a considerable ascent in the church towards the east. There are some open benches, with plain rude ends, and some irregular high pews, one of which is roofed. There are three bells. The font is too small. The churchyard is unusually extensive.

1867.—The church has been restored in excellent style and spirit by G. E. Street.

Llangurig (St. Curig).

A rude plain church, consisting of a west tower, nave, with narrow north aisle, and chancel with a small north chapel. The whole, both within and without, is very rude and rough ; the tower massive and strong. The windows are square-headed and Perpendicular. The aisle is very low as well as narrow, and is divided from the nave by two plain and wide Pointed arches springing from a square pier without moulding. The whole of the roof is of the rudest timber-work. The chancel arch pointed and rude; there are stone steps leading up to the rood-loft, and a large portion of the rood-loft screen remains, having pretty good carved woodwork and vine-leaf cornices. The font has an octagonal bowl, with some ogee panelling. The whole is singular from its rudeness.

Llanidloes.

1829.

This church has a west tower, nave, chancel, and north aisle. The tower is low and massive, with large flat buttresses, and is crowned by an ugly wooden belfry. A stringcourse is carried as a label over a plain west door. The north doorway is Early English, and has been a very good specimen; the arch is obtusely Pointed; the mouldings, unfortunately, are gone, but the shafts remain, and have very fine foliated capitals. The walls are of rough stone, and rather rude appearance. The nave is very lofty, and divided from the aisle by five extremely fine Early English arches, having excellent mouldings resembling those of Wells Cathedral; the piers are formed of fine clustered shafts, the capitals of which have foliage quite equal in execution to those of Rievaulx Abbey or Lincoln Cathedral. The roof of the nave is a very good open one; the collars form an obtuse arch, between which and the ridge is pierced tracery, and the hammer-beams rest on angel figures bearing shields. The aisle has a plain timber roof. The windows are Perpendicular, chiefly square-headed, plain and Late; that at the east end of five lights. The aisle is co-extensive with the nave and chancel. The font has an octagonal bowl panelled with quatrefoils, rather small on a slender stem, set on two steps. From the churchyard is a very pleasing view over the Severn, with wooded hills and verdant meadows.

Llanwnog (St. Gwynog).

October 26, 1855.

This church in general appearance resembles that of its neighbour, Aberhavesp, but contains more objects of interest. It is a single body, without aisles, and at the west end one buttress, with a Pointed belfry of wood over the west end. The east window is Perpendicular, of three lights, and has a head corbel at the apex externally; the other windows are modern and bad. The great feature of this church is the fine rood-loft between the nave and the chancel, which is in fair condition, of Late Perpendicular character, with much panelling and open-work to the loft itself. The screen somewhat resembles that at Llananno, in

Radnorshire. There is a piscina on the south of the altar. The chancel has a panelled ceiling. The font has a plain octagonal bowl, on a stem of the form usual in the neighbourhood. The rood-loft is approached by stone steps on the north, within the church, which are not as usual in a projecting turret, but run straight along the north wall, unprotected.

1866. A restoration has been effected and new roofs put on. That of the chancel has a ridge externally; there is the original boarding in the chancel roof, coved and ribbed, star fashion, with bosses. The masonry is rough sandstone, at the east end new pointed. Some new Perpendicular windows replace the former bad ones on the south. On the north are two Decorated new windows. The seats are new and open, and there is an organ in the chancel. The belfry has been rebuilt, and stands on upright posts, in the interior, which look too slight. Some of the original stained glass, with a figure of St. Gwynnoc, is collected in a north window. The rood-loft and screen remain complete, though rather rickety. The loft has the usual vine-leaf cornices, with Tudor flowers, and has panelling, alternately plain and sculptured; below the loft is open tracery, and the *quasi* roof with ribs and bosses; these latter have letters. The overlaping cornice is supported on wood posts, and in the centre is the door, with pierced spandrels. The west side is the richest; but the east also has panelling.

LLANWRIN (ST. WRIN).

September 6, 1852.

An undivided church without aisles, with a south porch and small bell-turret over the west end. It is rather wider than most of the neighbouring churches, and entirely of Late Perpendicular work. The walls are whitewashed, the roof a long unbroken one of slate. On the south side is one single-light window, with a kind of trefoil head. Most of the windows are square-headed, of two lights, but that at the east end is a large Perpendicular one of five lights with transom, by no means bad in in its tracery, and containing stained glass, now much mutilated, in which may be discovered the Crucifixion and the Blessed Virgin and Saints. There is a Perpendicular wood screen between the nave and chancel, of rather plain work, having in the centre a wide door, and on each side seven compartments with trefoiled arch heads and pierced spandrels. The roof is of a common pattern, with rude quatrefoils in the timbers. In the chancel it is rather better finished. There is a west gallery, and several very plain, rude, open benches, but the whole is neater than usual. The font has a plain octagonal bowl on a stem of like shape, set on a square base. The porch is large and very plain. The north wall leans. On the altar-rails is a Welsh inscription, with the date 1709. The churchyard is very pretty, with a large yew tree, and is entered by a lych-gate.

Penegos (St. Cadvarch).

September 9, 1856.

A small church, with low tumbledown walls, and of one space without distinction of chancel. Over the west end a slated belfry. The roof is of open timbers; the windows all bad modern insertions, except perhaps one slit on the north wall of the chancel. There is an arched recess in the south wall. The font has a small, rude octagonal bowl, on a square base. The church is pewed and out of repair, but kept neat. There is a large, plain, south porch, and a lych-gate to the churchyard.

Archaeologia Cambrensis.

SIXTH SERIES.—VOL. I, PART IV.

OCTOBER, 1901.

NOTES ON THE OLDER CHURCHES IN THE FOUR WELSH DIOCESES.

BY THE LATE SIR STEPHEN R. GLYNNE, BART.

(*Continued from p.* 147.)

DIOCESE OF LLANDAFF.

GLAMORGAN.

Aberdare (St. John).

June 1, 1849.

This church is scarcely worthy of notice, being so entirely modernised. It has a nave and chancel, the arch of which is Pointed, and a south porch. A small belfry over the west end. There is not one original window remaining, but the old font is extant: a large octagonal bowl, entirely plain, upon a stem of similar form.

Barry (St. Nicholas).

September 9, 1866.

A very small, mean church, externally whitewashed, roof and all. It has a chancel and nave, and over the west end a bell-cot for two bells in open arches. The chancel arch is flat, plain, and diminutive. There is a south porch. The font is octagonal and modern, and the windows have all been modernised. In the churchyard is the stump of the cross-shaft.

Bishopston.

July, 1836.

The church is prettily situated in a deep hollow, amidst rocky hills and embosomed in trees. It consists of a west tower, a nave, chancel, and south porch. The tower very rude, having a coarse battlement with billet cornice under it. No buttress or divisions, and the openings extremely narrow and rude—more of the castellated style. Within the porch is a doorway, with semicircular arch upon imposts. The chancel arch is low and pointed, but with very slight curve. On the north side of the nave, near the chancel arch, is a very small trefoil lancet, set obliquely in the wall, and looking towards the east. On the south side is a wider lancet, also with trefoil head. The chancel has on the south one single and one double lancet, entirely plain. The interior is very bare, but with modern pews. The old font has vanished.

Cadoxton-juxta-Barry (St. Cadoc).

September, 1865.

This church has a chancel and nave without aisles, a south porch and western tower, the whole of the outer walls being whitewashed. The tower is without buttresses or string course, rather low and rude, having a saddle-back roof with gables, a projecting-stair turret at the north east, a Perpendicular two-light west window, the belfry openings small and slit-like, and one single-light trefoiled with label. The porch is very large, and the interior doorway has continuous moulding. Probably the whole church is Perpendicular; the roofs are of cradle form. The chancel arch is Pointed and quite plain, without impost. The windows on the south of the nave are square-headed, of three lights, labelled; and there is a projection corresponding with the rood-loft's place. On the north side of the nave is a narrow window near the west, possibly Norman; and near the east end are two tiers of small narrow windows (lychnoscopic?), the lowest a mere slit; the upper with trefoil head. The chancel has no window on the north, but on the south a Perpendicular square-headed one of two lights, with a label. The east window is modern and poor. In the churchyard are the steps of the cross.

Cadoxton-juxta-Neath (St. Cadoc).

August 17, 1869.

A large church, almost completely modernised, save the tower. It has a spacious nave and chancel, but no aisles, and seems to have been enlarged and widened; the outer walls apparently all modern, and having poor Gothic windows, some of which contain coloured glass. The chancel arch is perhaps original, obtusely pointed, plain and low; on each side of it, in the wall, opens a smaller arch, not similar in size or shape. The chancel has some curious, but not very ancient, monuments. The tower at the west end is of the local type, strongly-built and plain, approaching a military character. It is without buttresses, and has one string, an embattled parapet, and corbel table. The west window, of two lights, verges from Decorated to Perpendicular, its hood on head corbels with a bishop at the apex. The west doorway has bold continuous mouldings and hood. On the south side a pointed door leads to the stair-turret, which only extends up part of the tower. The belfry windows are trefoil-headed, single lights, and some other openings are mere slits. The tower appears to be vaulted within.

Caerau (St. Mary).

September 27, 1848.

A small church on an abrupt eminence, where was a Roman encampment. It consists of a nave and chancel, west tower, and south porch. The tower is small, of rude construction, with pack-saddle roof, having the east and west sides gabled. The belfry windows long and square-headed, and a few other slits for openings, and some traces of a west door. Against the north wall of the tower are some rude steps. On the north side this tower has no opening whatsoever. The porch is large, and entirely vaulted in stone; its doors very plain. On the south side of the nave is a window, formed of two trefoil-headed lights. On the north, near the east end of the nave, a low single, labelled window with trefoil feathering, apparently Third Pointed. The tower opens to the nave by a low Pointed arch. The chancel arch is Pointed and continuous. The chancel has some square-headed windows of two lights, of debased character. The font has a cylindrical bowl on a shaft of like form. On the north side of the nave is a stone bench. The walls are whitewashed.

Coychurch (St. Grallo).

September 25, 1847.

A fine church and unusually good; cruciform, with central tower; the nave having aisles and clerestory. There is both First and Middle Pointed, plain but good, with much of the Herefordshire character, and comparatively little damaged by modern alterations. Some parts are Transitional in character. The windows of the aisles are lancets, with trefoil heads, opening internally by a segmental arch. The west window of the nave has three lancets within a containing arch; and below it is a First Pointed door with hood-moulding and shafts, which have bands and moulded capitals. At the west end of each aisle is a very curious window, in shape of a quatrefoil, presenting to the interior the shape of a lozenge. These are said to occur in some other churches of this county, but are certainly very rare. The nave and aisles have sloping roofs, covered with stone slates. The nave is lofty, but narrow. On each side is an arcade of four lofty and bold Pointed arches, with octagonal piers, which have been scraped. Beyond the eastern termination of this arcade is an unusually large interval of masonry on each side. In that on the north is a staircase leading to the belfry, and carried over part of the north aisle, where it is lighted by small square-headed openings. This staircase also communicates with the rood-door, and the entrance to it faces west. The clerestory on the south has six-foiled windows, just seen externally over the aisle roof. On the north the windows are closed. The roof of the nave is coved and ribbed with a panelled cornice, having small figures of angels. The four arches under the tower are Pointed, springing straight from the walls without shafts. The transepts are lower than the nave, and have flat roofs. The north transept has at the end a First Pointed triplet within a segmental arch; the corresponding window on the south is Late and poor. The arch between the north transept and the aisle is Pointed, but very coarse. In the south transept a stone seat extends along the south end. On its east side are two trefoiled lancets; and on the jamb of one is the figure of a saint painted in ancient fresco, but the head has perished. In the south wall is a piscina, with bold hood. The tower is embattled, and has the usual Welsh corbel-table, which, though appearing at first sight First Pointed, is probably much later. The belfry windows are square-headed and labelled. There is a sort of dormer window at the east end of the north aisle, where the tower staircase is. The chancel is advanced First Pointed, but has a flat panelled ceiling to all but the eastern bay, which is coved. The arrangement of the chancel windows is elegant; on each side are four trefoiled lancets, set closely, and opening internally by segmental arches; and beneath them is a stringcourse. One window on each side is hidden by a modern monument. The east window is Middle Pointed, of three lights. Under the south-east window is a Pointed piscina and a sedile, each surmounted by a pedimental canopy. Under the north-east window is a large Pointed aumbry. There is a priest's door, and appears to have been a sacristy on the north. On the north side is a rudely-sculptured effigy of an ecclesiastic, with this inscription: "Here lieth in grave the bodi of Thomas Ivans, Clerk, Person of Coychurch, demised the 2 day of April Anno Dom. 1591." Opposite to it, on the south, is a diminutive figure of the same style, probably commemorating a child. "Here lyeth the bodi of William sonne of Robert Thomas and Barbara Fleming his wife." The chancel is left free from pews. The walls have been scraped, and much remains of ancient colouring discovered; on the southern tower arch some of Arabesque pattern, very bright. The font has an octagonal bowl on a stem of like form. The south porch has a good ribbed roof; within it is a door with good First Pointed mouldings, and near it internally is a benatura of circular form. The chancel has externally a First Pointed corbel-table, and there is a similar one in the transepts. The hoods of the windows are connected externally on the chancel and south aisle, but on the north aisle are no hoods. In the churchyard are some curious ancient crosses; one, near the east end, has only the shaft remaining, of square form, and ornamented with fretwork. Near the south door is a more perfect one, with an octagonal shaft covered with fretwork; the cross itself is perfect, and also fretty.

Coyty (St. Mary).

September 25, 1847.

A cruciform church without aisles, but with central tower; the nave is very wide, and the transepts are equal in height to the nave; the whole appears to be Middle Pointed, plain, but in many respects good, and not unlike Coychurch in its character; the tower, indeed, is almost a counterpart of that of Coychurch, with the usual Welsh corbel-table under the battlement, square-headed two-light belfry windows, labelled, and a slit below. There is a plain south porch, with stone benches and a timber roof. The west door is plain, chamfered; the west window is a large and fine one of five lights, with rather curious Middle Pointed tracery: something of a sort found in Kent. On the north of the nave are three windows of two lights, set deep with a double arch, which are also Middle Pointed; on the south two similar ones and one square-headed Third Pointed. The transept ends have each a three-light Middle Pointed window; those on the east side of the transepts are of two lights without foils. There is a kind of billet corbel-table along the exterior of the chancel. The roof is open, plain ribbed, and of cradle form. The tower rises on four Pointed arches, without capitals, opening to the nave, chancel, and transepts. Under it is a groined ceiling octopartite; it contains six bells. Over the west arch are stone brackets in the bare wall. In the north transept is an ogee three-foiled piscina in the eastern angle, and along its western wall are some rude stone steps leading to the tower and to the rood-loft, supported upon two stone semicircular arches; beneath is a stone bench and a Pointed recess in the wall. The chancel has a three-light east window, which seems to have been altered, and is of a poor kind. On the north are two small Middle Pointed two-light windows, and an appearance of a hagioscope. At the south west a plain wide lancet, not brought down low; another at the south east, under which is a curious arrangement of piscina and sedilia, consisting of three cinquefoiled arches with hoods, the two eastern set up very high, the western carried down low as a sedile. In the eastern is a multifoiled piscina; and in the pavement below it is a drain. There is a little bracket in the east wall. In the south transept is a trefoiled piscina, with cinquefoil orifice in the south wall. The font is a very large octagonal bowl without stem. On a flat stone is a cross, and near the south door a small arched recess, probably a stoup. Another similar one is near the west door. In the north transept is a small effigy of a female. In the chancel is an elegant panelled wood chest, exhibiting some fine carving, chiefly Flemish.[1] The churchyard is unusually large, and closely adjoining it are the ruins of the castle, much overgrown with trees and ivy.

Eglwys Brewis (St. Brice).

July 24, 1871.

A small church, having only chancel and nave, south porch, and a small bell-cot over the west end. The chancel arch is Pointed, but very rude; and adjacent to it are stone blocks, facing west on each side; and on the north is some indication of a door to the rood-loft. There are no windows on the north side. The east window has two trefoil-headed lights, which seem to be Perpendicular. On the south of the chancel is an oblong recess and a priest's door. The font has a circular bowl on steps, with rope moulding round its upper part. The south porch has a Pointed doorway; within it is one with obtuse arch, and near it an octagonal stoup. The bell-cot is original, and of uncommon character, square and embattled, with a corbel-table, and a niche for a bell.

Flemingstone (St. Michael).

September 27, 1848.

A small church, consisting of a nave with south transept, a porch and a chancel. Over the west end of the nave is a gable for two bells in open arches. The porch is set very close to the west end of the nave, and has a wood roof, and a stone seat on the west side only. The outer door is continuous, the inner door cut in the centre. At the west end is an obtuse lancet, now closed; and in the south-west part of the nave is a small window, with obtuse arched head and hood-moulding, having three-foil feathering. The transept is very large in proportion to the church, and has a

[1] Described and illustrated in *Arch. Camb.*, 5th Ser., vol. v, p. 400.

three-light window of Third Pointed character; and on its east side a single trefoiled window with ogee head. In the wall of the transept is a fine sepulchral arch, with mouldings and shafts of Middle Pointed character. At the west end of the nave is a stone bench. There are no original northern windows, but one modern one. The roofs of both nave and chancel resemble that at St. Mary Church; that of the nave is plainer, and that of the chancel has the eastern portion boarded. The chancel arch is a rude, misshapen one, bulging out, and without mouldings. The east window is of two lights, square-headed, with label. On the south of the chancel is a priest's door, and two single windows with obtuse trefoiled heads, one of which has mouldings. There is a rood-door at some height on the south side of the chancel arch. The font has an octagonal bowl, on a stem. The exterior walls of the church are whitewashed, according to the practice of the neighbourhood.

Gileston (St. Giles).

July 24, 1871.

A small church, prettily placed close to the mansion-house, and comprising nave and chancel only, with south porch. Over the west end is a small square-topped bell-cot, embattled like that of Eglwys Brewis, and set on corbels. The chancel-arch is Pointed, but very rude; within it is a plain wood screen of Perpendicular character. There are no windows on the north. On the south are two square-headed windows of two lights, one Decorated, one Perpendicular in character. At the south east of the nave are two small two-light windows, set one over the other, and probably connected with the rood-loft. On the north is also a door, perhaps belonging to the same. The chancel has an east window of two cinquefoiled lights, labelled and square-headed; at the south west a single light trefoiled; one at the south east is a trefoiled lancet. The west door is closed. The interior is pewed, but neat. The font has a circular bowl on a similar stem. The porch is large in proportion, and has stone benches. The doorway is Pointed, and over the interior one is a niche with ogee crocketed canopy. Near this door is an octagonal stoup.

KENFIG.

September 26, 1848.

A rude church of the South Wales stamp, comprising a nave and chancel, with a large and coarse western tower, to the west side of which is attached a very large porch. It is probable that the whole is Third Pointed, though there is little distinction of an architectural character. The tower is much ruder than that of Pyle; it has a battlement, below which on the north and south sides is the usual plain corbel-table; but none on the east or west. In the centre of the western battlement is a kind of pediment, a common feature in this country. The belfry is lighted only by a narrow slit on each side; on the south is a large stair-turret, lighted also by slits, but not reaching up very high; some of these slits are barred. The tower arch is low and plain, rude, and misshapen, of very obtuse form upon coarse imposts. The chancel is also very low; there is a square recess on the north-east side, and brackets in the east wall. The font is Norman, and curious; the bowl cup-shaped, with a rope moulding round the rim, and courses of scaly mouldings. The whole church is whitewashed externally, even the roof. The site is elevated, and commands a sea view over flat sandy burrows.

LALESTON (ST. ILLTYD).

September 24, 1847.

Chancel and nave; south porch and large west tower. The chief features seem to be Third Pointed; but the windows throughout the chancel and nave are modern, and closed with shutters. The chancel arch is depressed, and rises at once from the wall. On each side of it is a niche in the wall; that on the south moulded and trefoiled; that on the north without foils. The interior is rather bare. South of the altar is a piscina, being a sort of trough beneath a Pointed arch. There are large monuments against the east wall. The tower has rather more architecture about it than usual in the district, though partaking in some measure of the prevalent character. It is large and massive, without buttress, with battlement and the usual corbel-table. It is divided by a string into two equal portions, and another string runs round the base. At the south-east is a large embattled stair-turret, and at the angles four gargoyles. There is on the west side a door, with rather flat arch, moulded, and flanked by pinnacles, which rise from the corbels. Over it is a three-light window, with rather unusual, but not elegant, tracery of six foils, apparently late. The belfry windows are double, and square, on each side. The lower story of the tower is vaulted, and the arch to the nave springs from shafts, being of good Pointed form. On the north side of the nave, near its east boundary, is a large projection, with window in it, now closed; this is, perhaps, the rood-stair. Most of the northern windows are closed. The south porch has curious pinnacles flanking its gable, and one at its apex. These are of rather debased work, but vary, and stand upon very odd corbel-heads. Within the porch is a depressed ogee door, with finial mouldings and small shafts. The font has a plain, small, octagonal bowl on a stem of like form. There is an ugly west gallery.

Llancarfan (St. Catwg).

July 24, 1871.

This church is larger and of greater interest than most of those around. The plan comprises nave and chancel, with south aisle reaching to the east end, western tower and south porch. The nave is spacious;

and the aisle, which is nearly equal to it in width, does not extend quite—though very nearly—to its western extremity. The arcade of the nave to the aisle has four sharply-pointed Early English arches, springing from square piers, with angles chamfered; the caps have rude sculpture of varied character; some have foliage or fruit; one has four rude heads; and the arches are perfectly plain and without mouldings, all of rough execution. The roof of the nave is of cradle form, with ribs and bosses; and those of the south aisle and chancel are similar, with plastering between the ribs. The south porch is large and good, Perpendicular, with open-ribbed roof, and has a pretty good entrance-door, with arch mouldings and hood. Over the inner door is a Perpendicular niche, with a flat arch, trefoiled. The inner doorway is Early English, of rude character, the arch having rounds and hollows in its mouldings, and the inner member having a recessed column with fluted cap. Near this door internally is a circular stoup, also Early English. The windows of the nave and aisle are mostly Decorated, of two lights; on the north is one of two lights, Late Perpendicular. The chancel arch seems to be transitional from Norman to Early English, but is much mutilated; it is Pointed, and very wide, in a very thick wall; and the square imposts have a kind of Early Dogtooth ornament in hollow squares. The lower part of the archway is crossed by a dwarf wall, which must have supported the screen of the rood-loft. In the north wall, corresponding with the rood-loft's place, are two square-headed windows, each of two lights, and one above the other; the lights cinquefoiled, one having lighted the screen and the other the gallery. The door and stair to the rood-loft partly remain, and can be seen in the north wall: and there are two brackets above the chancel-arch. The chancel is spacious, and has on the north two windows: one Decorated, of two lights; the other of singular design, and probably Perpendicular, having five lights under

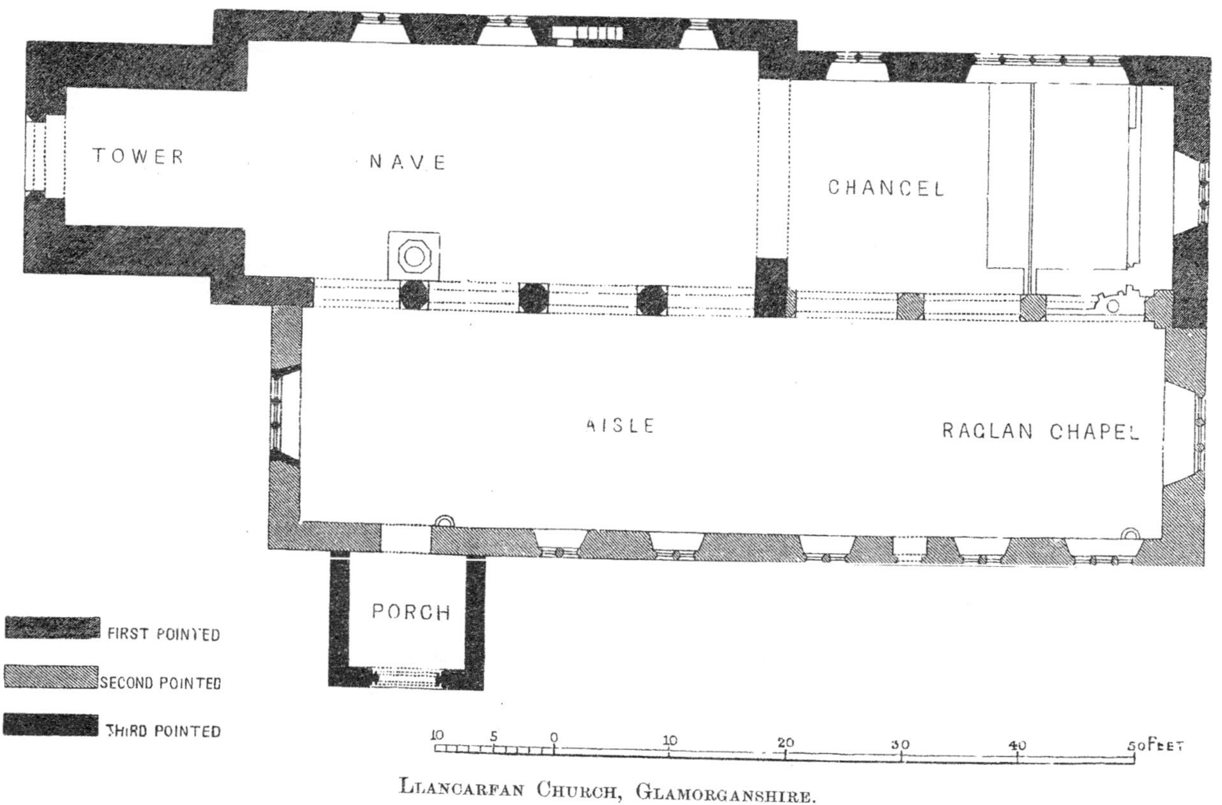

LLANCARFAN CHURCH, GLAMORGANSHIRE.

a Tudor arch, with tracery, all set in a square frame. The design is uncommon, and not elegant. The east window is of three lights, modern and poor; but the arch is original. There is an elaborate wood screen, in a decayed state, placed now as a sort of reredos, near the east wall, just enclosing a small space, by some supposed to have been across the chancel arch. It is really a fine thing: having nine spaces, with canopies of delicate tabernacle work, undergroined, set on a stone base. The chancel is divided from the south aisle, or chapel, by three Pointed arches, with octagonal piers having capitals. The arch is chamfered; in the eastern appears a stone bench, or rude piscina, and a piscina with a moulded circular bowl. The south aisle is carried on, without division, to the east end; but the part ranging with the chancel is considered to be the chapel of the Raglans. There is some Perpendicular wood screen work in the arcade, parting off this chapel. In the south wall is a round piscina in the cill of the south-east window. The windows are Decorated, of two and three lights; but one set up high in the south wall, and corresponding with those on the north connected with the rood-loft, which is Perpendicular, square-headed, of two lights. The font has an octagonal bowl, on a similar stem; and on each face a kind of tongue-like cutting, set on a square base. The tower arch is a plain Pointed one, upon corbels. The tower is of the prevailing half-fortified character, strongly built and rather low, with embattled parapet on small corbels. It has a modern west door and window; there are no buttresses nor string-course, and all the original openings are loop-like and single. The roofs are covered with slate. The interior is untidy and neglected, though some faint symptoms of restoration appear in the chancel. In the churchyard are two old buildings: a church-house of Perpendicular character, and the rectorial barn of earlier and better character.

Llandough (near Cowbridge).

August 18, 1869.

A small church, undergoing a complete restoration. It consists of nave and chancel, south porch, and bell-turret over the west end. The original chancel arch, said to have been very small and narrow, in a large mass of wall, has been replaced by a new Pointed one, upon marble shafts, and a new low stone screen has been added across it. The chancel roof is entirely new, as is also the east window, which is of three lights, Transitional from Early English to Decorated; the windows of the chancel are lancets, with trefoil heads, and the most eastern has two seats in the cill; there is a good piscina, with trefoil head on shafts. A new vestry has been added on the north, opening by three Pointed arches. The nave has an ancient cradle-roof;. and there is the arrangement common in Glamorganshire, a rood-door on the north, with the steps in the wall, and a low trefoil-headed window, set quite lŏw down. The windows of the nave are mostly new: but one near the west is original: a single lancet with trefoil head. At the west end is a two-light window, with trefoil heads, and no west door. The projection for the rood-stair is seen on the north; while on the south of the nave, near the east end, is an oblong recess, and a square opening filled with a quatrefoil, and a slit-like window set high. The porch has an obtuse arch to its doorway, and within it one of similar form; it has stone seats and a fair timber roof, with flowered cornices and a central rib. Near it is a stoup of circular form.

Llandough (near Cardiff).

August 8, 1853.

This small church seems to have been almost wholly rebuilt, and presents a neat though modern appearance. It has a chancel and nave only, with a bell-turret over the west end for two small bells.

The chancel-arch is Norman, with chevron mouldings upon imposts. There are no windows on the north: those on the south are square-headed, of Decorated character. The west window is of three, the east of two lights, all Decorated, and the latter has some stained glass. In the churchyard on the north side is a shaft with four corner columns, having Perpendicular lozengy mouldings, probably the remains of a cross.

Llanedarn (St. Edeyrn).

July 11, 1858.

A small church, having chancel and nave, western tower and south porch. The east window is Decorated, of three lights, but may have been altered from its original plan; north of the chancel is a single window, trefoiled. In the nave, on the north, is one of two ogee-headed, trefoiled lights (a local type); also some Perpendicular ordinary windows, both north and south, of three lights; and close to the pulpit on the south a small two-light Decorated window. There is a projection on the north for the rood-stair; the chancel-arch is Pointed, with continuous mouldings. The tower has a battlement, and a slight projecting staircase on the north; no buttresses, but the base swelling out with a batter. The belfry windows are of two lights. The tower-arch to the nave is Pointed and plain: the font octagonal and small. The porch has a moulded doorway. The walls are whitewashed externally; and the church stands conspicuously on a lofty eminence, just opposite the Church of St. Mellon's, on a similar height.

Llangan.

August 18, 1869.

It is doubtful whether any part of the present church is ancient: the whole seems to have been recently rebuilt, yet possibly some portions of the walls may be old. It has a chancel and nave, with south porch; and over the west end a bell-gable for two bells in open arches. On the north side may be seen the projecting rood-staircase, with the upper and lower doors opening within; the door has wood tracery; over the south door is a new canopied niche. The chancel-arch is Pointed, with continuous moulding, perhaps original. The west window is a trefoil-headed lancet: on the north is one window of two trefoil-headed lights; the southern windows are all new: the east window has three lights, with trefoiled ogee heads. The seats are all open; and there is a neat new font, in Norman style, having a circular bowl on an octagonal stem.

In the churchyard is a very fine cross, in perfect state; the shaft is lofty, and surmounted by a kind of tabernacle work, with four niches facing the cardinal points, containing sculpture representing: 1. The Crucifixion; 2. The Pieta and two other figures, north and south. There is also another round-shaped sculptured stone (cross), rather coarsely executed.

Llanmihangel (St. Michael).

August 12, 1869.

A small church, adjacent to the fine ancient mansion, consisting merely of nave and chancel, with south porch and western tower. The porch resembles that at Llandough, has an obtuse arch at entrance, roof open and ribbed, and inner doorway Pointed and chamfered. The tower arch to the nave is a rude and very narrow Pointed one, and over it a door opening to the ringing floor; the tower has plain vaulting, and a west window of Perpendicular character, square-headed and cinquefoiled, of two lights: it is small, and has a saddle roof, the east and west sides being gabled; a corbel table under the belfry windows, which are mere slits; no buttresses, but a Pointed doorway on the west, and much of the prevailing quasi-military character. The nave has a fair open roof; the wall-plate on the north comes down lower than on the south, and is on corbel heads. The windows are various. On the north of the nave is a trefoil-headed lancet and a square-headed window, set high, close to the rood-loft place; also one below it, labelled, but partially closed. There is the rood-door and staircase in the wall, as at St. Donat's. There is an oblong square-headed window on the south, and a square-headed Perpendicular one of two cinque-foiled lights. The chancel arch is a rude obtuse one; the chancel is short, the east window square-headed, of two lights, debased: the north and south windows modern, and the walls wainscotted in debased style. It has two large monuments, 1717 and 1722, to the Edwins.[1] Near the chancel arch are two brackets. The font has a square bowl with the angles cut off—a common practice hereabouts—on a short stem. In the churchyard, close to the east end of the chancel, is a curious sepulchral slab, on which is sculptured the bust of a priest, sunk in a hollow, with clasped hands, below which is a cross; the inscription is not very legible. The work is rude, and the date appears to be 1591. Curious as a post-Reformation specimen of a Roman Catholic priest.

Llantrithyd (St. Illtyd).

September 27, 1848.

The plan is that of a nave, chancel, west tower and south porch; the chancel lower than the nave. The tower tapers, and has a battlement and block cornice; the centre battlement on the east and west sides being gabled. The belfry window is a square-headed slit, and there is another slit for an aperture; no buttress nor west window; but a plain west door, with mouldings; and hood, with corbels. In the north wall of

[1] Humphrey Edwin, Lord Mayor of London, bought Llanmihangel from Sir Robert Thomas about 1650, and his heiress married Francis Wyndham, *unde* the Earl of Dunraven.

the nave is an arched recess, under which is a sepulchral effigy in low relief, with the hands crossed over the breast, and holding something resembling a pear; and round the edge of the slab is a course of ball-flowers round the base, something like the Tudor flower. On the south side of the nave are two Middle-Pointed windows of two lights, set on different levels, one with a hood: on the north one of two lights without foils, and one doubtful lancet; the roof of the nave resembles that at St. Mary's Church. In the south wall, near the pulpit, is a trefoiled niche. The chancel arch has pretty good continuous mouldings; the framework of the "Sanctus" bell may be seen within it. There is a rood-screen of Third-Pointed work, having a cornice of Tudor flowers. The chancel is debased Third-Pointed, and has a labelled priests' door on the south, and square-headed windows. The east window is of the Laudian kind, resembling those at St. Catherine Cree in London, with the date 1655. In the sacrarium is a slab, sculptured with a cross as late as 1588; and in the chancel a very gorgeous Elizabethan tomb to some of the Basset and Mansel families, A.D. 1597. The font has an octagonal bowl, and is sculptured in a debased fashion, probably coeval with the chancel, with crosses and roses.

In the western portion of the nave, on the south side, is a trefoiled lancet, and over it a debased square-headed window. The porch has a plain Pointed inner door. The exterior is whitewashed. In the churchyard is a *dos d'âne*, with a cross. On the west side of the church is an Elizabethan mansion.[1]

LLANTWIT-NEXT-NEATH.

May 31, 1849.

A small church, having a nave, chancel, west tower and south porch; rude and plain. The chancel has a trefoil-headed lancet on the south, but the east

[1] For an account of Llantrithyd Parish Church and Mansion, see *Arch. Camb.*, 3rd Ser., vols. xii. and xiii, and vol. xv.

window is closed, and there are none on the north side. Those in the nave are modernised. The chancel arch is rude and obtuse. The tower is decidedly a Welsh one, plain and rough: but, like many others, probably Late, though with features that might appear earlier. It has no buttress but a battlement, under which there is the common block cornice. The belfry windows are square-headed; the lower part of the tower bulges out, a frequent characteristic in South Wales. The font is square, with rope moulding round the upper part.

Monknash.

August 11, 1869.

A small church, having chancel and nave, with south porch, and bell-cot over the west end; the latter is stepped. The east window is Decorated, of three lights; and on the north of the chancel is one single Norman window. On the south of the nave are square-headed, labelled, Perpendicular windows. The chancel-arch is a plain one of semicircular form; and across it a low, plain, stone screen, which is original. The porch is very large. The church has been restored, and is in good case.

Newcastle (St. Illtyd).

July 26, 1860.

This church had originally only a nave and chancel, with west tower; but the nave has lately been rebuilt, and has received the addition of a north aisle. The chancel is old, and rather mean outside, though neat within; and has a lancet on the north side; a very diminutive east window of two lights, Decorated, having externally a mutilated crocketed hood, windows of a similar kind on the north and south of the chancel, and on the south a single light, with ogee head and hood on head-corbels. The tower is left untouched, and is of the local type, of good masonry and strongly built; it seems to be Perpendicular, and is without buttress, divided by one stringcourse; has a battlement with block corbel table under the parapet, four small pinnacles, and an octagonal stair-turret at the south east, which rises above the parapet, and has itself a battlement and small pinnacles, and is lighted by small slit openings. There are gargoyles at the angles of the parapet of the tower; the belfry windows are square-headed, labelled, and of two lights: on the west side a three-light Perpendicular window and labelled doorway: the tower is of fine grey stone, and has a picturesque effect. The newly-rebuilt nave has Decorated windows of two lights; those on the north are single, with tracery on the heads; the porch has also been rebuilt; the arcade of the nave has three Pointed arches, with octagonal columns; the interior is entirely fitted with open seats, and the pulpit and desk face south. The font has an octagonal bowl on a stem of like form. The tower arch is Pointed, chamfered, and continuous. The chancel-arch seems to be new, and the chancel is modernised within.

The situation is fine: the churchyard, on an elevated terrace, commanding a pleasant view. On the north are the ruins of the castle, in which is a very curious arched doorway, apparently Transitional from Norman to Early English; the outer arch semicircular, with continuous roller-moulding, having foliaged capitals: within this arch is the doorcase, of a sort of segmental form; the whole enriched with a curious unusual ornament, resembling a series of clasplike articles.

Newton Nottage.

September 24, 1847.

A curious little church, quite on the sea shore, comprising only a chancel and nave, with a western tower and south porch. The chancel is regularly developed, and is narrower than the nave. The whole appears to be Third-Pointed, of a rough kind. The tower is remarkable: very solid and massive, and having the east and west sides of the parapet gabled, so as to form a saddle-back. The north and south sides are rudely embattled. Under the parapet is a corbel-table, set lower on the east and west than the other sides. In the east gable is a flattened trefoil opening. On the west side is a pretty good door, with ogee canopy, having crotchets and finial, and flanked by pinnacle buttresses. The finial of the west door is surmounted by a flowered cross, and under the flanking pinnacles are angels bearing shields. The arch mouldings are good, with small shafts set on stone ledges. Above is a three-light Third-Pointed window. There are some plain slits on the north and south sides of the tower. The tower arch to the nave is Pointed. The chancel arch is also Pointed, but plain and rude. Most of the windows are modernised. The roof is plain and open. On the north side of the nave, towards the east, is a projection containing the stairs, both to the rood-loft and pulpit. The pulpit is remarkable, being of stone, forming a semicircle: but decidedly Third-Pointed. It has a cornice, with bold sculpture of vine leaves and grapes; also a sculptured representation of the martyrdom of a saint, bound by the feet, between two executioners, one bearing an uplifted sword. The entrance to the pulpit is by a flattened arch, containing a flowered moulding and two figures of angels. The rood-door on the north has a flattened trefoil head. The chancel has on the south a labelled priest's door, and a debased window. The east window is closed. The altar has a very large stone slab on solid masonry. It is doubtful whether this is ancient. The east end is flanked by pinnacled buttresses. The south porch is very large, now used as a vestry, and contains a benatura, on a shaft. The door has a flat arch. The font has an octagonal bowl, on a diminishing stem and square plinth. The chancel has a coved roof. There is a gravestone, charged with a cross.

PENARTH (ST. AUGUSTINE).

August 8, 1853.

A small church, very conspicuously situated on an eminence overlooking the Bristol Channel, and well known as a sea-mark. It has only a chancel and nave, with a low west tower, and a south porch of large dimensions, as usual in this locality. The tower is gabled on the east and west sides; is thick and strongly built, according to the provincial character, with small openings or windows partially closed; the arch to the nave is very rude and plain. The chancel-arch is also very plain, and of depressed form; there are no windows on the north of the chancel: and those on the north of the nave are very small, with trefoil heads. The east window is of three lights, and poor character; on the south of the chancel is one of two lancet arches, but of doubtful character. In the nave on the south are two Late square-headed windows and one single one. On the south of the chancel arch is the rood-door, with steps in the thickness of the wall. The font is of a common South Wales type: the bowl square, scolloped below, stands on a cylindrical stem raised on steps. The south side has been white-washed externally. In the churchyard are two high steps, and the stump of a cross.

PYLE (ST. JAMES).

September 26, 1848.

The plan comprises a chancel and nave, with western tower and south porch. There is less than usual of the Welsh rudeness, but the whole appears to be Third Pointed. The east window is of three lights. On the south of the chancel are two square-headed ones, respectively of one and two lights, and a priest's door. In the nave are square-headed windows on the south side, with labels, and of two and three lights. On the north side were originally no windows, but some modern ones have been inserted. At the north-west of the chancel is a projection, with a door, apparently for the rood-stairs. The chancel arch is Pointed, springing straight from the wall; and the tower-arch is similar. The south porch has stone benches. The tower is solid and strongly built, embattled with corbel-table below the battlement. The belfry window on each side is a square slit; another slit in the stage below; and on the west side a square-headed window, closed; and a Pointed door. There is no buttress, but on the south a stair-turret, reaching up one story. There is a cross in the churchyard.

EGLWYSILAN.

May 17, 1851.

A long, narrow church, on a lofty eminence, with only a few houses near; the chancel is somewhat lower than the nave, and there is a south porch and western tower; the latter is plain and rude, with battlement and four small crocketed pinnacles, but no buttress; it has two stringcourses, and few openings; on the west no belfry window: on the other sides square-headed. There are very few windows on the north side of the church, and those modern; on the south of the nave are some square-headed and debased; in the chancel, on the south, are two trefoil-headed lancets of First-Pointed appearance: and at the east a triple one cinquefoiled, perhaps Late and altered. The chancel arch is a plain Pointed one, rather straight-sided. There is a stone bench along the south wall of the chancel. The west door is modern, and the porch plain. There is a lych-gate.

LLANTRISANT.

May 16, 1851.

A church superior to the generality in the neighbourhood, and lately improved in condition: it consists of chancel, nave with aisles, western tower, and north and south porches. The exterior is whitewashed, and of plain Third Pointed character; but within the remarkable feature is the simple Norman arcade on each side of the nave, of five plain arches, tall and wide, with plain cylindrical columns, having square

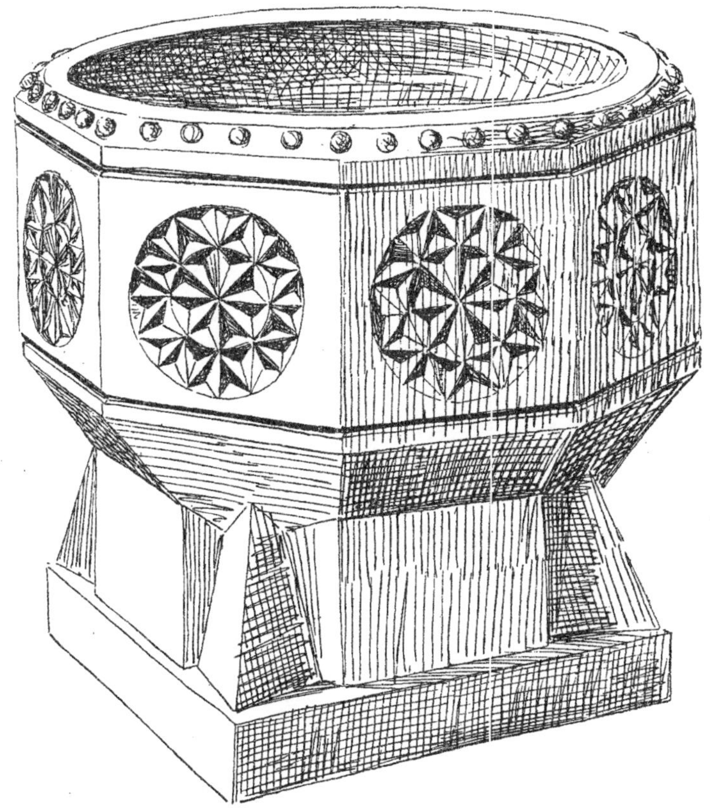

Font in Llantrisant Church, Glamorganshire.

caps of thin laminæ. The aisles are very narrow, with lean-to roofs; that of the nave a respectable open one, of a plain sort and Welsh character. The seats are all low and uniform: the pulpit a new Gothic one of wood. The chancel is low and mean; its arch low, but rather acutely Pointed. The tower arch is Late and depressed, with continuous moulding. There is a vestry, parted off at the west end of the south aisle.

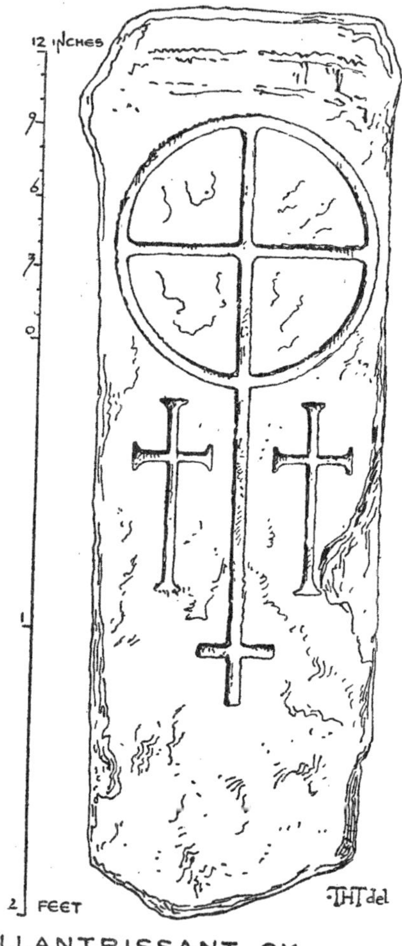

LLANTRISSANT CH.

Sketch of Slab, with Incised Crosses, fixed into North Side.

The font has an octagonal bowl, each face having a circle containing stars; the stem an octagonal block. Against the north wall a sepulchral effigy of a lady is set up, in fair preservation. The windows are mostly debased. The tower is low and embattled, with square-headed belfry windows and corner buttresses, and an octagonal corner turret. The situation of the church is very striking: on the summit of a lofty hill, surmounting the mean old town, and commanding a transcendentally-fine view. The graves are very prettily adorned with flowers.

PETERSTONE-SUPER-ELY (ST. PETER).

August 31, 1849.

This church has a nave and chancel, south porch, and western tower: chiefly Third Pointed, and white-washed externally. The tower is large, with a battlement and gargoyles: the usual Welsh corbel-table and buttresses at the angles; it is divided by a stringcourse into two portions; the belfry windows are square-headed and labelled; the west window similar; the tower has a stone vault, and the arch is Pointed and continuous, with much blank wall about it. The roof is open, the timbers on small wood shafts, all of Late character. The windows of the nave are square-headed, and of three lights. The porch is large, with a plain door, on which is some old ironwork. At the south-east corner of the nave is a square-headed window of two lights, set high up in the wall. The chancel is lower than the nave; the chancel arch Pointed and chamfered, springing straight from the wall. On the south are the rood-door and steps, but the rood-screen has been destroyed. The east window is modernised: on the south of the chancel is a priest's door, hooded, and a square-headed window of two lights; no windows on the north. The font has an octagonal bowl, rather small, upon a shaft with horizontal mouldings.

St. Athan.

July 24, 1871.

A cruciform church, with central tower and no aisles. The roofs high-pitched; and there is a large south porch. The west window is Decorated, of three lights, rather Transitional to Perpendicular. There are no windows on the north of the nave or transept. The The tower is upon four very plain Pointed arches, without moulding or imposts. The north transept has on the east a three-light window, merely of plain lights under a Pointed arch; at the north end is a square-headed debased window of four lights, with transom. The windows on the south of the nave have been mutilated; but at the south-east is set high up a narrow single window, as if connected with the rood-loft. The south transept is altogether Decorated, and has at the east and west a square-headed window of three lights. There is a hagioscope from the nave into the south transept, and one from the south transept into the chancel. The window at the south of the transept has externally an ogee crocketed canopy upon corbel-heads. At the south end is a fine one of three lights, with reticulated tracery; and there are squints from this transept into both chancel and nave. Under the south window are two fine tombs to the Berkerolles, formerly possessors of Orchard Castle, in this parish. One is under a fine ogee canopy, with crockets and finial flanked by crocketed pinnacles, set diagonally, and having double feathering: the larger canopy divided into two arched divisions, with central corbel. The eastern pedestal of the pinnacle bears an ogee niche, with piscina, showing that this was a chantry chapel, with an altar. The western pedestal is also charged with a fine canopied niche, with good groining under the canopy, and roses in the mouldings, carried all down. The tomb is panelled with ogee niches, having crockets and intermediate pinnacles; and from it are the recumbent effigies of a knight and lady; the former, cross-legged, bears a shield charged with a chevron between three crescents, and a dog at his feet. The lady has a wimple; and both have the hands joined in prayer. Another tomb, beneath a crocketed ogee canopy, has also two figures, of a knight and lady: the knight cross-legged, with shield having the same armorial bearings as the other. The details are similar to those of the other sepulchre, and there are flanking pinnacles.[1] The chancel has a Decorated east window, of two lights, restored; at the south-east one of two trefoiled lights; other windows on the south are single lancets, much splayed. There is a priest's door on the south, and a Pointed niche south of the altar, with piscina. In the north wall is a sepulchral recess. The font has a circular bowl, cup-shaped, with projecting lip, and on a square plinth. There is a staircase in the north transept, leading to the tower, and perhaps the rood-loft. The porch is large, and has a ribbed wooden roof; the outer doorway Pointed and continuous; the door within stilted. The tower has battlements, and corbel-table below, and corner buttresses.

St. Bride Major.

August 26, 1849.

The plan is chancel and nave without aisles, west tower and north porch. The north door and the chancel arch are Norman, both rather curious, the north-door head being a kind of flattened trefoil under a semi-circular tympanum. The north porch is of very large size, as is often the case in this county; and near the door is a benatura. The most frequented approach to this church is, contrary to usual custom, on the north, on which side is the shaft of the Cross, elevated on several steps. The chancel arch is a plain semicircular one, with square imposts, which have very regular

[1] For a full description of these tombs, see *Arch. Camb.*, 3rd Ser., vol. xv, pp. 76-77.

mouldings. On each side of the arch is a hagioscope, with flattened arch; and on the north angle of the chancel is a recess. The chancel has on the south three lancet windows, with trefoil heads; and one at the north-west. The other windows throughout the church are wretched modern ones. There is a very small, plain piscina on the south. In the north wall of the chancel is a large Third Pointed tomb under a flat ogee arch, with flowered mouldings, statues and shields, the sides enriched with kneeling figures in relief, and four crocketed canopies. The effigies represent a cross-legged knight and lady, of the Butler or Boteler family.[1] There is also an earlier slab, with the inlaid figure of a crossed-legged knight, with inscription to John de Boteler; and also another slab, with a cross, in the two upper spaces of which are crosses within circles. The font is a plain octagonal. The tower is vaulted internally in its lower story, and opens to the nave with a continuous Pointed arch; it resembles many neighbouring towers, and is of doubtful age, having a battlement and the Welsh corbel-table, and incipient angular pinnacles and buttresses; a stair-turret on the south, only to the lower stages; and a square-headed belfry window.

St. George-super-Ely.

August, 1857.

A small cruciform church, with central tower, and having no aisles. There is a lancet window on the north of the chancel; the other windows are mostly modern, and the church has of late years been much renovated. The tower itself has been raised, and gabled on each side; but rises on four very plain Pointed arches, opening to the chancel, nave, and transepts.

[1] For a fuller notice of this church and its monuments, see *Arch. Camb.*, 5th Ser., vol. v, p. 395.

St. Hilary.

August 17, 1869.

A good parish church, in excellent condition, and having more of good work than the generality of churches in Glamorganshire. It consists of a nave with south aisle, chancel, western tower, and south porch. The nave is unusually wide; and the whole of the roof, both in nave and chancel, is new, with tie-beams and king-posts. The porch is also new. The chancel arch is Norman, has two-edged orders on imposts, and is very obtusely Pointed; the arcade of the nave has five Pointed arches, with mouldings carried down the piers, which have no caps. The windows of the nave and aisle are all Decorated, mostly renewed; on the north side one is Pointed, but almost all the others are square-headed, except the one at the west end of the aisle, which is a Perpendicular of five lights. The chancel has on the north side one single lancet, singularly running externally into an ogee-head. The east window is flowing Decorated, of five lights; the south-west window a narrow, square-headed slit. There is a square-headed piscina in the east wall, and a bracket. On the north-east of the nave are two stories of windows connected with the rood-loft; one set quite low, the upper one square-headed and of Decorated character, with two lights. The rood-steps remain in the wall. The font has a cylindrical bowl of Early character. The seats are all open, and the internal arrangements very satisfactory. In the north wall of the nave is a sepulchral effigy of a lady wearing gloves. There is also a good effigy of Sir Thomas Basset, A.D. 1423. The south doorway has an obtuse arch, with continuous mouldings; and near it is a stoup. Over it is a half-octagonal bracket for an image, enriched with flowers and shields. The tower opens to the nave by a continuous moulded Pointed arch, and has an embattled parapet and corbel-table, and corner buttresses. The west window is square-headed, of three lights, Perpendicular; the belfry windows square-headed, of two lights, and labelled; and a west door with Pointed arch. In the churchyard is a cross on high steps, well restored; the churchyard is beautifully kept.

St. Lythan.

August 28, 1849.

A small church, containing chancel and nave, a chapel south of the former, and a western steeple. The tower is small and very plain, without buttresses, and has a saddle-back roof, but scarcely any architectural details. The openings are mere slits. The proportions of both chancel and nave are small; the chancel arch a very small and rude Pointed one, and above it two brackets; the tower arch is Pointed, and entirely plain. There were originally no windows on the north, but some modern ones have been inserted: on the south is one single trefoiled window, and one square-headed, of two lights, of Third Pointed character. The east window in the chancel is Middle Pointed, of two lights, now much mutilated; on the north side of it is a rude niche: on the south a bracket. The south chapel is Late Third Pointed, having small square-headed windows; it is divided from the chancel by two singular flat arches, springing from a central massive circular pier, with capital; the character is very singular, and probably provincial and debased. The roofs are open, and very plain. The font is Norman: a cylinder moulded all round with chevrons. Within the south door is a benatura.

St. Mary Church (near Cowbridge).

September 27, 1848.

The plan comprises a nave and chancel, with west tower and south porch; the chancel being much lower than the nave, and divided from it by a flat and ugly arch. There is here some improvement on the usual Glamorgan character of churches. The nave has only one window on the north, a trefoil-headed lancet; the other windows are square-headed, mostly of debased character, without foils; but that at the east end has cinquefoil feathering. In the east wall is a projection, with a small piscina; and on the north of the east window an ogee-headed niche. The roof of the nave is open, and rather a good one, with collar and flowers along the ridge; the timbers forming compartments nearly triangular in shape, and the cornice embattled. The eastern bay of the nave has the roof boarded, with small wood shafts. The chancel roof much resembles that of the nave, the eastern part being boarded. The south porch has an open wood roof, and within it is a benatura, of a sort of cushion shape. The font has a cylindrical bowl, with a moulded string round it, upon two square steps. The tower is plain, with a battlement but no buttresses; and under the parapet a small corbel-table. The belfry windows are square-headed, divided by a mullion; other openings are square-headed slits. On the south side is a square turret, with small grated apertures. The tower arch is rude, and rather obtuse. The west door is Pointed, and over it is a small square-headed two-light window; the centre-piece of the battlement on each side is gabled. On the north-east side of the nave is a projection in the wall for the rood-steps. The chancel inclines very considerably to the south. The steps to the cross in the churchyard remain.

St. Nicholas.

September 27, 1848.

A coarse church, with much of the local character, and rather curiously arranged. It has a nave, chancel, south chapel and porch, and western tower. The south chapel extends along the whole chancel and part of the nave, as far as the porch. The tower seems to be rough

Third Pointed, with strong, thick walls and battlement, under which is a corbel-table of the usual sort. The belfry window is of two lights; there is a west door, and the base bulges out, as often seen in the towers of Wales and Devonshire. The porch has a cross on the gable, and over the inner door a niche. In the western part of the nave is a three-light Third Pointed window on the south; and there are two of the same kind on the north side, with transoms. There is another three-light Third Pointed window at the west end of the chapel, encroached upon by the porch. The south wall of the chapel was rebuilt in 1803, and contains ugly Italian windows. The chancel arch is Pointed, springing straight from the wall: and the tower arch to the nave is like it. The nave opens to the south chapel by a Pointed arch, with mouldings, having a Middle Pointed character, springing from clustered shafts. The chancel opens to the same chapel by a rude, misshapen arch of great width, and without mouldings; and has a debased north window and an ugly one of Strawberry Hill Gothic at the west end. The roof of the chancel is open, with an embattled cornice. On the south side of the sacrarium may be seen a great curiosity: the original Sancte bell, in a perfect state, but without inscription. There is a modern vestry on the north side of the nave. The altar-rails are carved in Jacobean style. The font has an octagonal bowl upon a stem.

Sully (St. John Baptist).

September 9, 1866.

A small church, in pretty good case, and situated in a beautiful churchyard full of flowers and dressed graves. It has a nave and chancel only, with western tower; the latter is of the South Welsh character, rude and strongly built, with neither string nor buttress, but a swelling base; has a battlement, with corbel-table, slit-like belfry windows, and a lancet on the west. The chancel is nearly equal in length to the nave; the chancel arch is a wide Pointed one, without imposts. The tower opens to the nave by a plain, low door-arch. There are no windows on the north; all those on the south and east are Perpendicular: the east window is of three lights; those on the south square-headed and labelled. There is a priests' door. In the chancel is a piscina, set very far westward, with moulded arch and good mouldings, and a shelf. The church is pewed.

TYTHEGSTON.

September 24, 1847.

A small church—chancel, nave, south porch, and western bell-gable. The whole apparently Late. Several of the windows are bad insertions; but the eastern a two-light Third Pointed one. The chancel arch is depressed, of Tudor form, and low, with continuous mouldings. Over it is a great expanse of bare wall. On the north side of the chancel is a single narrow slit, walled. The south-east window is closed; but in it is a low seat. The priests' door is also closed. The porch is rude. The font has a circular bowl, the base like a reversed cup.

WENVOE (ST. MARY).

September 9, 1866.

This church has a nave and chancel, south porch, and west tower; the body much modernised, and in great measure rebuilt. The chancel arch is plain Pointed, possibly original; there is also a Pointed doorway (perhaps old) within the porch. The tower is old, and has no buttresses; but a plain battlement, with corbel-table; the belfry windows are plain rectangular; other openings mere slits; west door plain Pointed, with label. In the churchyard on the south are the steps of the cross; the churchyard is prettily planted with flowers.

Archaeologia Cambrensis.

SIXTH SERIES.—VOL. II, PART II.

APRIL, 1902.

NOTES ON THE OLDER CHURCHES IN THE FOUR WELSH DIOCESES.

BY THE LATE SIR STEPHEN R. GLYNNE, BART.

(*Continued from vol. i, p.* 278.)

MONMOUTHSHIRE.

ABERGAVENNY (ST. MARY).

July, 1836.

THIS has been a very large cruciform church, of which the eastern portion, comprising the choir, central tower, and transepts remain unaltered, but the western portion has been rebuilt in a very poor modern Gothic style, and not in a line with the eastern part. The exterior even of the choir is much modernised; the tower is massive and embattled, with a square turret at its north-west angle, the belfry windows Pointed. The western part alono is generally used for service, and is pewed and galleried in the fashionable style, and contains a good-sized organ. The chancel is completely excluded, but apparently used for the administration of the Holy Communion. The tower rises upon four lofty Pointed arches, which seem to be of simple Decorated character. Those on the north and south are on imposts with the ball-flower; the eastern and western on corbels formed by heads of saints and bishops. The chancel is lofty, but without a clerestory; on each side are two curious straight-sided arches, springing direct from plain flat piers, and forming the divisions of the aisles. The roof of the chancel is groined in modern plaster work. The windows are Perpendicular; those at the east end of the aisles are of five lights, with some painted glass—that at the east end of the chancel is of four lights—those in the side of the aisles are of three lights, of a plainer description. There is one Decorated of three lights on the north side; the south transept is used as a school. The choir contains some elegant wood stalls and desks, with beautiful canopies and cornice of vine leaves; but the most conspicuous feature is the abundance of fine sepulchral memorials in the choir and its aisles, though some of these are much mutilated. In the south aisle, beneath a window, is some elegant panelling in stone, with niches of ogee canopies containing tracery, upon which, on the sill of the window, is the recumbent effigy of a cross-legged knight, with a sword by his side and a dog at his feet, in excellent preservation. Another tomb is of late date, panelled with ogee canopied niches, painted and gilt, and containing angel figures, surmounted by an ogee canopy, and in the back of the arch bas-reliefs, representing figures kneeling on helmets and shields, and angels crowning the Virgin Mary. The effigy is of alabaster, representing a knight. Near this is a very large recumbent effigy, with head on pillow and an angel at the head. In the middle of the choir is an alabaster altar-tomb, on which are figures of a knight and lady beneath canopies, painted and gilt. On the sides of the tomb are niches containing saints. There is also another tomb in similar style, also with a male and female effigy, and another plainer and more mutilated. Another is of earlier date, evidently Decorated, and presents two smaller effigies, one at the foot of the other, a knight and a lady, the former having a shield charged with three fleurs-de-lys, and a cornice of foliage running round the tomb. There are some more effigies in a shattered state. In the south arch is a trefoiled niche with drain. The font is Early, the bowl of cup form, with rope-moulding round it.

Bassaleg (St. Basil).

This church has a west tower, a nave with south aisle, south porch, and chancel of plain and coarse work, chiefly Perpendicular. The tower is embattled, and divided into three stages by stringcourses; on its north-east is a square turret. The west door is late Perpendicular; over it is a square-headed window; the other openings in the tower are rude and square-headed. The nave and aisle are of equal height, and slated externally. The tower arch is a plain Pointed one; the south porch large, but quite plain. The nave and aisle are very wide, and divided by five singularly flat arches, with square piers having imposts. From the very remarkable shape of these arches, it may be doubted whether they are original; there are, however, some specimens nearly similar in form in parts of South Wales and Monmouthshire, in which a rude and peculiar style certainly prevails. The windows of the nave and aisle are mostly deprived of their tracery; but this seems to have been Perpendicular; one at the west end of the aisle retains its tracery of this character, and at the east end is one of three lights, which seems to be of poor Decorated style. There is a projection on the north side containing a family pew. The pews are large, modern, and ugly. The chancel arch is not in the centre of the nave, and springs abruptly from imposts in the wall. The chancel has a Perpendicular east window of four lights, not very good, and some square-headed ones on the south. On the north side is a chapel, now closed. There is a large modern monument in the chancel, to Lady Morgan of Tredegar, *obiit.* 1808, with portraits in sculpture of her seven children. The east window contains painted glass, executed by the daughter of the Vicar. The font is cup-shaped, and appears modern. On the south side of the church, and quite detached, is a small

Perpendicular chapel of plain character; with the east window of three lights and the roof, ribbed in shape of arch.

Caerwent (St. Stephen).

This church has a west tower, a nave, and chancel; the former of which has had a south aisle, the latter both north and south aisles. The tower is Perpendicular, of excellent masonry, but plain and without buttresses. It has a battlement, an octagon turret at the south east, and square-headed belfry window, with tracery and lattice-work. On the west side a plain door and small window; the other openings small and square. There is a large north porch of two stories, the arch of entrance finely moulded, with small shafts having capitals, and one course of moulding flowered. The chancel is large, and about equal in length to the nave; the chancel arch good Early English, having excellent mouldings and clustered shafts, with good capitals, but clogged with whitewash. The nave has had a south aisle, of which the foundations are seen. In the wall are seen two plain Pointed arches, without mouldings, large buttresses being inserted on the piers. A wretched modern window is inserted in the wall. The chancel was divided from its south aisle by three very flat arches, like those at Bassaleg, springing from imposts on square piers. The north chapel of the chancel has been long destroyed, and a square-headed Perpendicular window inserted in the wall of division, which externally has a flattened arch and good mouldings. The east window is of two trefoil-headed lancets. On the north side of the nave is a Perpendicular window, with good mouldings. Near this church are remains of the ancient ivied walls, of the Roman Station.

Caldicot Church.

A handsome structure, with more good architecture than is usually found in this neighbourhood. It consists of a nave with north aisle and south porch, a chancel, and a tower situated between the chancel and the nave. The features are chiefly Decorated and Perpendicular. The porch is very large and fine, having an embattled parapet, but not quite completed; the entrance by a lofty arch, with rich mouldings springing from shafts, and crowned by a fine ogee canopy with crockets and finials, and flanked by buttresses with crocketed pinnacles. In the space between the arch-head and the canopy is some elegant sculptured foliage. Within the porch are stone seats on each side, and a row of head corbels. The doorway within it has a depressed but well-moulded arch, near which is a benatura, and above it a niche, with three-foils on shafts containing the image of a saint, apparently Decorated in style. The porch is set further eastward than usual, and in its angle is a staircase in a turret, which was intended probably to conduct to an upper story. The west doorway is Perpendicular, of plain but good work; near it is a trefoil-headed benatura on the exterior. The west window is of three lights, and may perhaps be of Decorated style. In the north aisle all the windows are uniform Perpendicular, of three lights. On the south side is one something resembling that at Caerwent, with square head, and rather elegant and singular in its tracery, evidently Perpendicular. The nave is spacious, and divided from the aisle by five Pointed arches, springing from light lozenge piers with hollow mouldings and small shafts attached. The tower is lofty and very plain, of Perpendicular character, having square-headed belfry windows of two lights, and a moulded parapet with Pointed roof of tiles. It opens to the nave and chancel by two plain Pointed arches, springing straight from the walls. The chancel is Perpendicular, its east window of three lights; on the south a small door, and on each side two windows; one on the south has something of a castellated character, with a kind of flattened trefoil-head of two lights. The others are square-headed. The chancel has a coved roof, plastered. The font has an octagonal bowl on pedestal of like form. There are a few pieces of stained glass. In the wall of the porch is an effigy, inserted in the wall but mutilated. The porch is superior in work to the other parts of the church.

CHRIST CHURCH.

May 7, 1849.

A large church, situated on a lofty eminence, and almost entirely Third Pointed. It comprises a nave and chancel, with wide aisles, a tower at the west end of the south aisle, and north and south porches. There is some trace of First Pointed work in the chancel; the tower is of rude provincial character, probably later; but within the south porch is a Norman doorway, plain, but late in the style, with a chevron moulding, a head at the apex of the arch, and the inner member rising from shafts which have knobbed abaci; the outer member appears to be a Third Pointed addition. The arcades of the nave have five bays: they are of Third Pointed form, frequent in the west of England, the piers of lozenge form with shafts attached, and intermediate hollow mouldings. The roofs are coved, with ribbed compartments. There is no clerestory. All the windows are of three lights, except the eastern one of five, the western of four, and a small lancet at the north-east of the chancel, which projects beyond the aisles and bay. This lancet has mouldings externally, and very fine ones internally, upon shafts. The chancel and the chancel aisles are all divided from the nave and its aisles by Pointed arches; that to the chancel is a fine one, with good mouldings and shafts. The others are without shafts. The rood-door is seen on the south, on the last pier adjacent to the chancel arch. On the same pier, facing south, is a small mutilated niche. The chancel and its aisles have lower roofs than the nave, but the general style is similar. On each side of the chancel the arcade consists of two arches and a half one (towards the west); the piers are lighter and smaller than those of the nave. At the east end of the south aisle is some good Third Pointed panelling against the wall, which seems to have been a reredos, it has two large octagonal projections, which appear to be the pedestals of niches. In the same aisle is also a labelled ogee piscina, with shelf. There is a projection externally in the north, corresponding with the rood-loft's place. The north porch is closed; both north and south porches are large and plain. The west door is closed also. The tower is a very large one, without parapet, but a rude block cornice at the top. The belfry window on the north is of three lights, labelled; there are several other openings in the tower, some mere slits, some arched, one with pierced quatrefoil stone lattice-work. It has no buttresses. The font is a plain octagonal one. There is a small organ, probably with barrels, and uniform pews. There is a piscina in the chancel.

DIXTON (ST. PETER).

September 27, 1847.

The plan is a nave and chancel, of some length, but without aisles; a north transept, north and south porches, and a western tower with short spire. The church is long and narrow, the tower is small, without buttresses, and appears to be First Pointed. The parapet is plain, the belfry window on each side a trefoiled lancet, under which is a string. On the west side is a lancet window. On the north side are some two-light windows, which appear to be Third Pointed; the south is one which seems Middle Pointed. There is a trefoiled lancet on the north of the chancel, and at the south-west of the same a square-headed slit. The other chancel windows are Third Pointed. On the south of the chancel, externally, is a stone bench, and the priest's door is closed. The chancel arch is a plain, low, Pointed one. There is a chamber connecting the north porch with the transept, lighted by a slit, and now used as a vestry. The interior is neat but pewed the whole has been recently restored, and has a modern look. The crosses at the gables have been renewed. The porches have lancet windows. In the churchyard are two circular bowls, now catching water, which must have been fonts on stumps. That which is now in use has an octagonal bowl, far too small. The situation is lovely, close to the Wye, with enchanting view of woody hills, and the spire of Monmouth, not more than a mile distant, is a beautiful object.

Llandilo Crossenney (St. Teilo).

October 16, 1858.

A fine cruciform church, with aisles to the nave; central tower with tall shingled spire, and a north aisle to the chancel; also a large western porch. The cruciform plan is somewhat lost by the conversion of the north transept into a chapel, and extending it, undivided, in the form of an aisle to the east end of the chancel. There are portions of all the three Pointed styles. There is a single lancet at the west end of the south aisle. The nave is lofty, with open roof and clerestory; has on each side a good arcade of four tall Pointed arches, springing from octagonal columns with capitals. The clerestory windows are Perpendicular, square-headed, of two lights. In the aisles, the windows are of Decorated character, square-headed, of two lights. The whole church has recently been restored, in a plain and satisfactory manner, and put into excellent repair. The nave is fitted with plain open benches; the font also is new, and the pulpit. The tower rises on four remarkably low Pointed arches, having continuous chamfered arches without capitals, above which is a considerable space of walling. The northern arch is made double, and strengthened by the addition—evidently an alteration of the original plan—of a work of solid construction, ranging with the arcade north of the chancel. There is a squint through this, and at the south-west of the chancel appear the doors that communicated with the rood-loft. The chancel roof is coved, but there are tie-beams moulded and foliated, and an ornamental cornice. There are varied Decorated windows on the south of the chancel, one of three lights, plain without foliation; one square-headed, of three lights, with external label. The east window is modern, of three lights, imitating Decorated tracery. On the south is a fine piscina with label and finial, and bold cinquefoil feathering. Between the chancel and the north chapel are two dissimilar arches. The western is well moulded, and rather straight-sided in the Herefordshire fashion, varying from Early English to Decorated, with good clustered shafts having capitals and base-mouldings. The eastern arch has been connected with a tomb, has plain continuous mouldings, and there is an opening through the pier. There is a rude oblong opening from the north chapel to the chancel, near the squint. The east window of the chapel is Perpendicular, of four lights; on the north is one wide lancet, and one two-light Decorated. At the west end, a good Decorated one of three lights. The north chapel of the chancel is now thrown into the transept, probably by a subsequent alteration, as appears by the strengthening of the north arch of the tower. The south transept has no large windows, but plain ones of two lights, unfoliated. Below the steeple are seen internally strong timbers, connected with the spire for the purpose of strength. There are six bells. The west window is Perpendicular, square, of two lights, and set high up. The porch is very large, and without much feature. The font is new, as also the pulpit. In the churchyard is the tall shaft of a cross, and a pretty gravestone, in the midst of creepers, to the son of Colonel Clifford.

Llandogo (St. Odoceus).

June 4, 1849.

This church is greatly modernised, the nave wholly so, and having a north aisle, divided from it by a modern colonnade : this aisle is probably an addition to the plan. The chancel is original ; has trefoil-headed single lancets on the north-east and south-east, and at the east end a double one, also with trefoil heads. The chancel arch is of questionable form, and is cut by the north wall : probably a modern alteration. The chancel has a priest's door on the south, and the south porch of the nave appears to be original, but of ordinary character. The churchyard is beautiful, and the surrounding views most lovely.

Langua.

1836.

This is a very small church, in a beautiful situation near the Monnow. It has only a nave and chancel, without a dividing arch, and a small turret over the west end. The windows are square-headed and Late ; on the north side there are none at all. The font is a cylindrical bowl on a shaft of like form, with square base.

Llantylio Pertholey (St. Teilo).

July, 1836.

This church is a rude and irregular structure, comprising a nave with aisles and a tower, and chapel on the north side, a chancel with north aisle, and a south chapel. The exterior is whitewashed ; the tower very plain, with belfry windows of two lights. There is also a south porch, in which is a benatura. Some windows are square-headed and of Late character, but there is one Decorated of three lights at the east of the north aisle. The south aisle is narrow, and divided from the nave by three very dissimilar arches, the first from the west lofty, the second lower, the third very rude. and with scarcely any curve, the first pier octagonal, the others quite plain. On the north are two arches, also dissimilar, both Pointed, but one much wider than the other. The nave and north aisle have waggon-roofs, divided into panelled compartments. There is a chapel added on the north side, which opens to it by two very flat arches in wood, springing from an octagonal pier enriched with fine moulding, and panelled, and the arches feathered. These must be of very Late and almost debased period. There is a similar arch in wood, opening to the chapel on the south of the chancel. On the north of the altar is a very curious small chapel of irregular form, opening by a low arch, and having a stone vaulted roof. The font is a plain octagon.

Llanvapley (St. Mabli).

August, 1861.

This church has a nave and chancel, south porch and west tower, and is situated in a retired churchyard, shaded with fine trees. It follows the Monmouthshire type. The chancel has on the north and south a single lancet window, and a double lancet at the east end, over which is a cinquefoiled circle. There is on the south an Early English piscina, with trefoil arch and double basin ; in the east wall two arched recesses and a bracket. The roof of the chancel is coved and ribbed. The chancel arch is Pointed, very rude and plain. The nave has its windows, square-headed and Perpendicular, of three lights. The roof of the nave is coved and ribbed. There is a projecting rood-turret on the north. The font has a circular bowl, with indented moulding round the upper part. The porch is plain, and has the openings of oilet shape. The tower is plain and strongly built, without either string-course or buttress. It has an embattled parapet, and plain block corbel table. The belfry windows on the north and east are mere slits, on the south and west they are double and Pointed. The west doorway is Pointed, and over it a modern window. The inner arch is plain rude Pointed. The roofs are covered with new slates, and in the churchyard is the base of a cross upon four high steps. The graves are covered with flowers.

Llanvihangel Pont y Moile (St. Michael).

May 8, 1849.

A small church, prettily situated, but much modernised, and containing very little worthy of observation. It has only a nave and chancel, a south porch, and belfry over the west end. The windows are chiefly poor modern Gothic, but that at the east end is an original Third Pointed one, of three lights. The door within the porch has a depressed arch. The chancel arch is a plain Pointed one, with continuous moulding. The chancel has its original roof, which is coved with ribs and bosses. The font is old : a small circular bowl, having in its lower part a kind of zigzag moulding, below which it becomes octagonal, of which form also is the stem. There is a stone bench outside the south wall.

Malpas.

May 7, 1849.

This curious small Norman church is in process of destruction. The nave has been unroofed and ruinated, but the chancel is not yet destroyed. The arch between the chancel and nave is rather a plain semicircular one, having on each side three large shafts with varied capitals, apparently not very early in the style; the abaci ornamented as well as the caps. The east window is a plain single Norman one. The north-east one is enriched internally with shafts having chevron mouldings and varied capitals, and a nail-headed hood. Externally, the windows are plain; below them is a string. That on the north of the chancel seems exter-

Malpas Church : View from West and Details.

nally to have its arch pointed, and the stone-work about it is singular and very irregular as to the shapes of the stones. The original flat buttresses remain. The nave has a curious and ornamental south door, the hood with spiral mouldings; the outer member with small chevrons, the inner one has a course of an unusual kind of ornament: each in bold relief, in form and general appearance not unlike a fan or shell. The shafts have on the capitals shallow intersecting arches. Under the Norman arch the door is formed into a double square-head, but it is doubtful whether this be the original arrangement. The windows are set very high in the wall upon strings, and all the buttresses are flat. Adjoining the church, on the south, are ancient buildings, now applied to farm purposes, which probably formed part of a religious house.[1] The nave is unroofed, but the walls still stand.

MAMHILAD.

May 8, 1849.

A small church, prettily situated on sloping ground, the churchyard containing some large yew trees. It consists of chancel and nave only, with south and west porches, and a bell-gable over the west end, with two open arches, and a wooden cage for the bells. The outer walls are entirely whitewashed. The work appears to be wholly Third Pointed. The west porch, now a vestry, is an original feature, somewhat unusual. The chancel arch is plain and coarse, but the chancel is properly developed. Most of the windows are square-headed, of two lights, with cinquefoiled heads. The east window is of three lights, and has some remains of stained glass, amongst which may be discerned the figure of a saint. There is a priest's door on the south, and no windows on the north of the chancel. The chancel roof is coved, with ribs and bosses and tie-beams. The south porch has an open roof, of cradle

[1] "The church was the chapel of a Cluniac establishment for two monks" (*Arch. Camb.*, 4th Ser., vol. x, p. 193), where J. O. Westwood describes and illustrates the church.

form, also ribbed. In the west gallery is some tolerable wood carving. There is an external stone bench on the south of the nave, as at Llanvihangel.

Marshfield.

July 12, 1858.

A long church, consisting of a chancel, a nave without aisles, a west tower, and a south porch. The latter, as usual in the district, is very large, and set further than usual towards the east. The outer doorway has good continuous mouldings, with flowered ornament, and flanked by pinnacles. Within the porch is an earlier doorway, of curious character, having a cylindrical moulding twined with branches, and shafts with capitals of foliage. Above it is a closed niche. The porch has stone seats. The chancel arch is Early English, with two orders of shafts, having excellent foliage on the capitals. The other windows are mostly Perpendicular, some of three lights, square-headed and labelled; one on the north of the chancel is a single cinquefoil-headed one. The east window, of three lights, has lately been restored. There are two windows at the east end of the nave, set high up to light the rood-loft. The upper and lower rood-doors also remain on the north side, where there is a slight projection. The nave has a ceiled roof, and is of great length; the western part divided off. The font is modern. On the north of the altar is a pointed recess. The tower seems Perpendicular, and of a local type, without buttresses and with a swelling base. There is a battlement, and a good west doorway which has two orders of continuous mouldings and hood. The west windows, of three lights; those of the belfry are of two lights, and square-headed. There is no projecting stair-turret. The tower arch is tall and open, with continuous mouldings. The churchyard is of unusually large size.

Matherne (St. Theodoric).

June 3, 1849.

A handsome church, with aisles to the nave, a fair chancel, south porch, and west tower. The latter and the external walls of the nave are Third Pointed; the chancel has some First Pointed features. The arcades of the nave are also First Pointed, but not quite similar. On each side are four arches. On the south, all segmental, the piers of clustered shafts with large moulded capitals. On the north, the three eastern arches are also segmental, but the piers are lower, and the capitals of the clustered shafts not so distinctly moulded. The west arch on this side is quite different; and, indeed, the form of that adjacent to it is quite changed by having been adapted to it. The west arch is low and very plain, nearly straight-sided, and its pier square, with imposts. The west side of the next arch is quite different from the corresponding one, and comes down straight to the square pier. The windows of the aisles are all of three lights, and pretty uniform. On the north the hoods are returned, and each pier between the windows occupied by two buttresses. On the south, there is only one in each pier. In the south-east angle there is the appearance of a rood-turret. There is no clerestory, the roofs sloping and tiled, without parapets. The chancel arch is a very plain Pointed one. The chancel has an east window of three lancets, which internally are included under a Pointed arch, and the window is filled with stained glass, in memory of the Rev. James Williams, late Vicar. This arch has a good cylindrical moulding. On the north side of the chancel is a single lancet, now closed, and all round the chancel is a stringcourse of the same character. The other windows of the chancel are Third Pointed, varying in character. On the south of the sacrariam is a wide moulded, arched recess, probably a piscina. There are two large projecting shed-like buttresses, one on each side of the east end, similar to those at St. Arvan's. The font is a small, plain, octagonal one. The south porch has its outer doorway with continuous mouldings and hood; the interior one rather similar, but with bases to the mouldings. The tower is of very good masonry, and lofty; of three stages, with battlement and octagonal turret at the north-east. There are small crocketed pinnacles and corner buttresses. The west door is plain; over it a small three-light window. In the next stage, a square-headed opening, ogeed with a shield on each side, charged with heraldic and other devices: in one appear the Arms of the See of Llandaff. The belfry windows are of two lights. The churchyard is beautiful and retired; adjoining it is the picturesque ancient palace of the bishops of Llandaff, now degraded into a farmhouse.

MICHAELSTON VEDW (ST. MICHAEL).

July 12, 1858.

This church has a nave and chancel, and south chapel or transept, western tower and south porch. The chancel is Early English, has on the south three lancets, now closed; at the east end a fair triplet with hood-mouldings outside, and pedimental buttresses at the angles. The chancel arch is Pointed and plain, springing at once from the wall. The south transept wall is partly modern. In the transept are Late square-headed windows, with labels. The other windows are modern. The porch is, as usual, very large and plain. The tower is embattled, with four short pinnacles, and the frequent corbel table under the parapet. The belfry window on each side has two trefoil-headed lights. The tower swells out at the base, and is without buttresses. The west doorway has continuous mouldings.

Mitchel Troy (St. Michael).

October 14, 1858.

This church has a nave, with south aisle, chancel, western tower, and south porch. There was formerly a north aisle, which is said to have been destroyed by the fall of the spire. The tower is very small, has a battlement, and a two-light Decorated window. The upper story of the tower overhangs. It opens to the nave by a narrow acute arch, with continuous mouldings. Within the nave there are arched recesses in the west wall, north and south of the tower arch. The nave has on the south a good arcade of three lofty Pointed, rather straight, arches, with mouldings continued down the piers without capitals. The western arch is lower than the others. There is a similar arcade in the north, but only two arches, that aisle not having been continued to the west end. The chancel arch springs straight from the wall. The east window is Decorated, of three lights. The windows north and south of the chancel are merely slits. The chancel is in good order. The altar has slate slab, with an incised representation of the *cœna* (*Domini*). The roof of the nave on the south comes low over the aisle. At the east end of the south aisle is a triple window, very oddly arranged, each light single and trefoiled, and gradually diminishing in height. In this aisle is also a rude piscina, with trefoil head. The churchyard is quite filled with trees and evergreen shrubs.

St. Patricio (St. Patrick).

May 19, 1864.

A very interesting little church, f. .m the ecclesiological curiosities which it contains. Its secluded but very beautiful position has probably been the cause of its having been so little disturbed. As a building it is not particularly remarkable, except for the curious chapel added to the west end. It has in great measure escaped

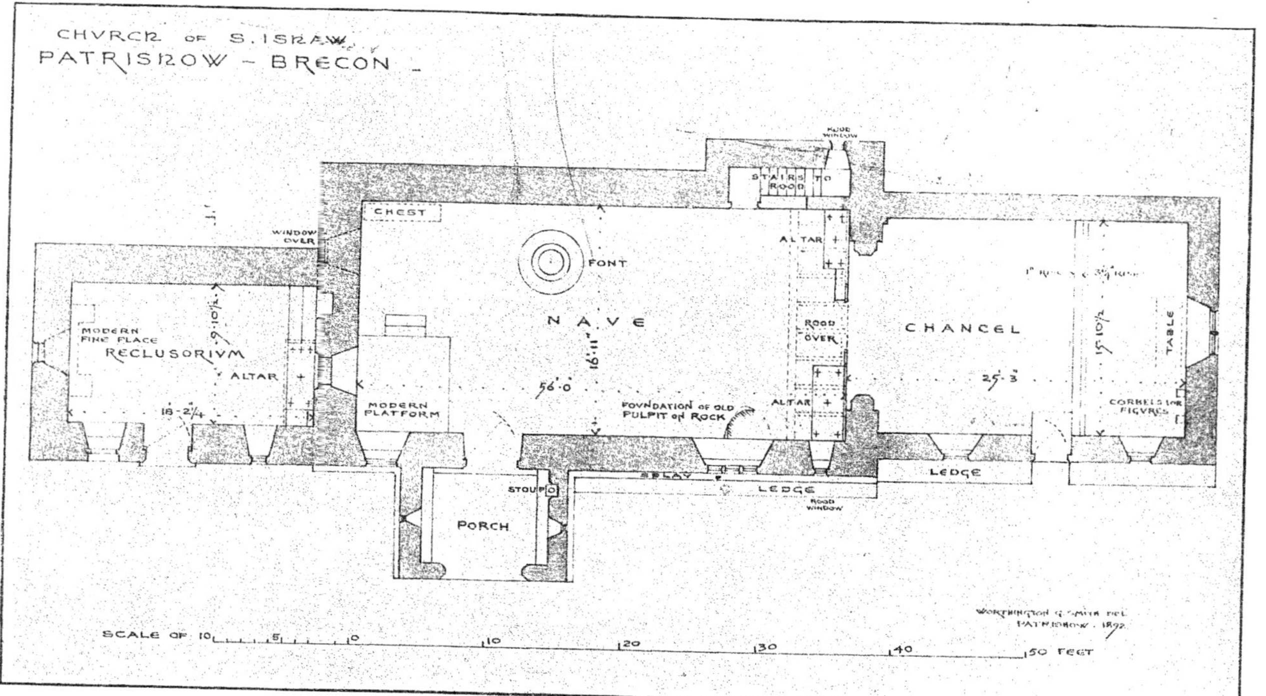

Ground Plan of Patricio Church, Brecknockshire.

Patricio Church (Exterior View showing South Porch).

Rood Screen and Loft in Patricio Church (West Side).

Rood Screen and Loft in Patricio Church (East Side).

Rood Loft in Patricio Church.

Cross-Section of Rood Loft in Patricio Church.

Interior of Western Chapel in Patricio Church
(View looking East).

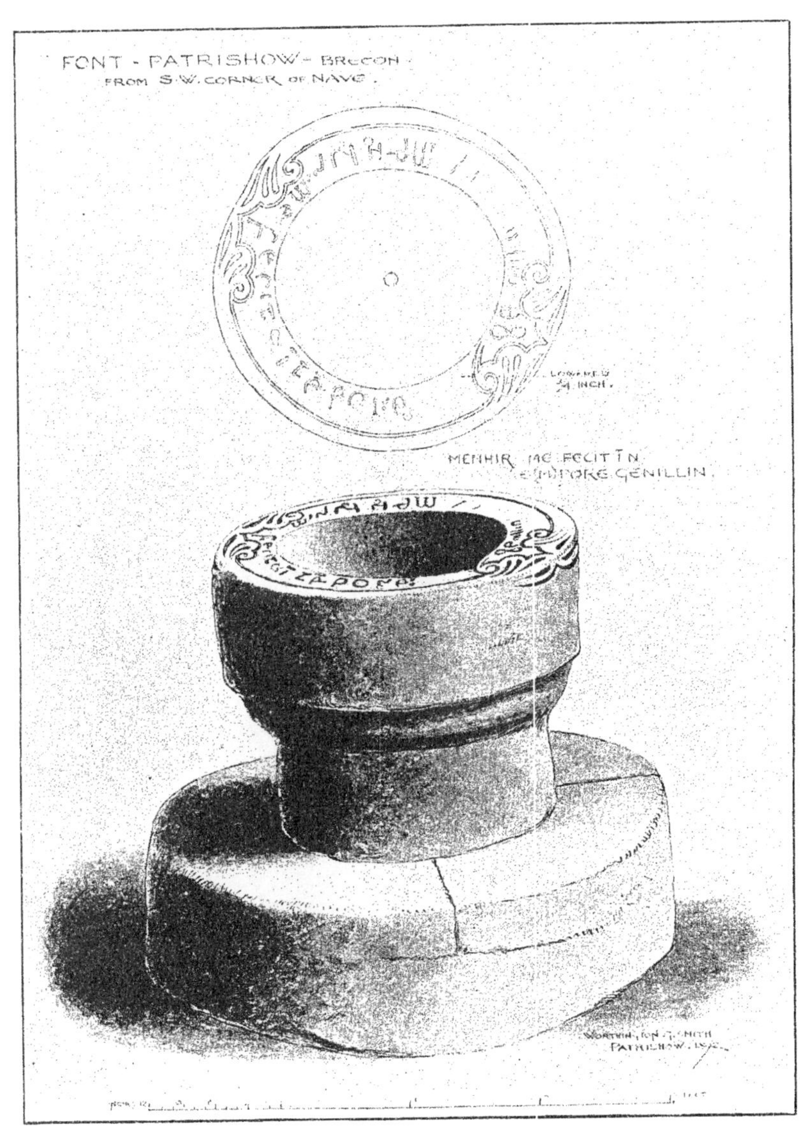

Inscribed Font in Patricio Church.

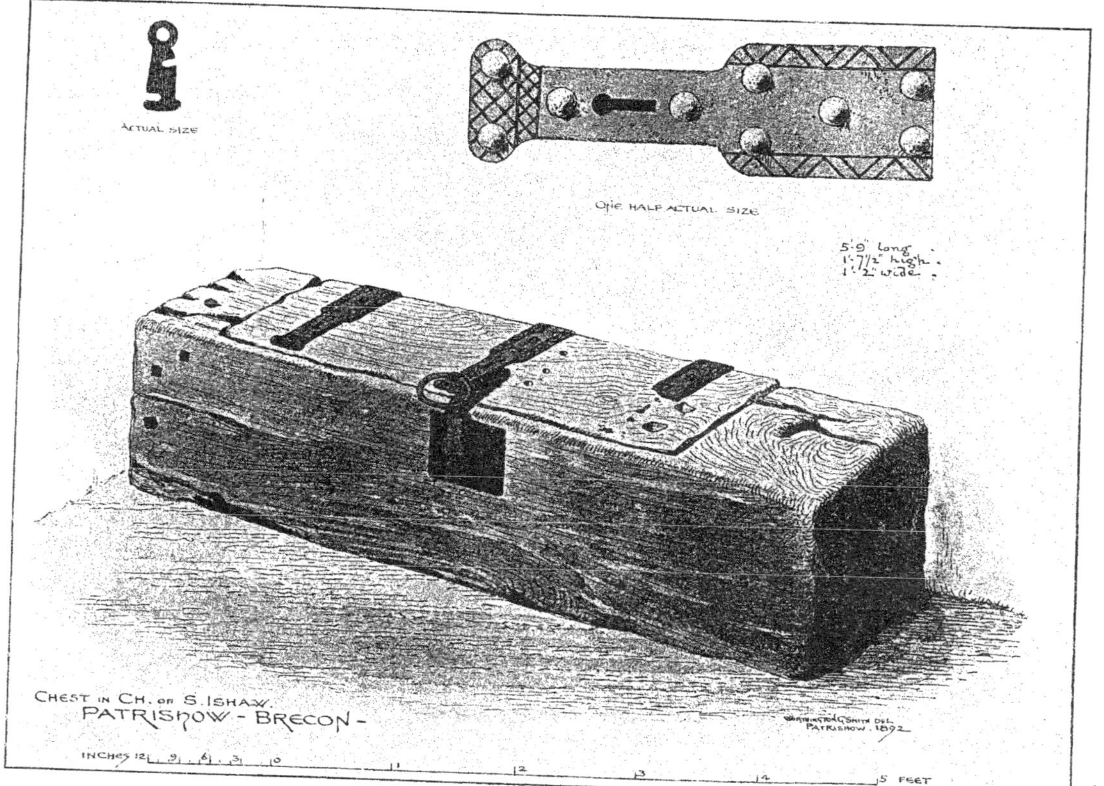

Chest in Patricio Church.

Holy Well at Patricio.

Patricio Church: Exterior View from the South-west, showing Western Chapel.

Cross in Patricio Churchyard.

modern alteration, but no part seems to be earlier than the Perpendicular period. The plan is merely a nave

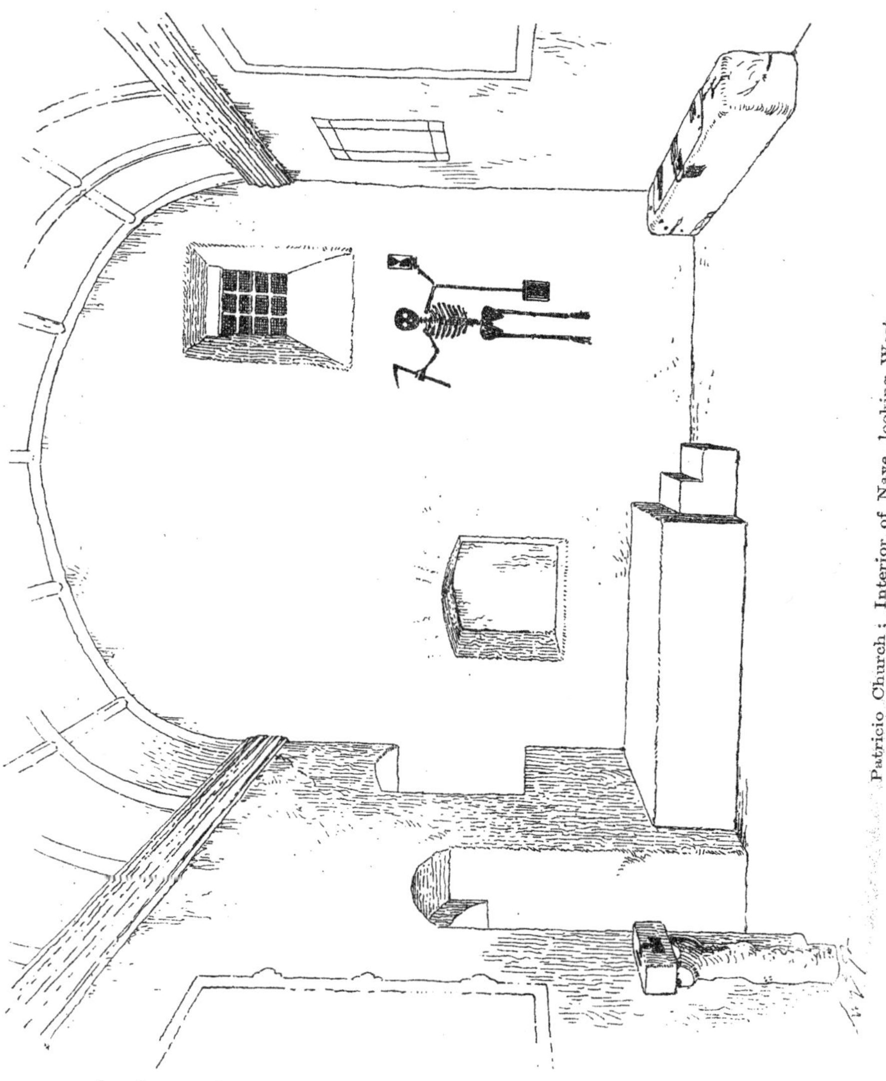

Patricio Church; Interior of Nave, looking West.

and chancel, with south porch and a western chapel added, but not open to the nave. Over the west end of the nave is a wooden bell-cot, for two bells in arches. The chapel, as seen from the south, seems as if it were a later appendage made, as is sometime the case, for a school. The whole of the exterior walls are white-washed. There are no windows on the north, which is often the case in small remote churches. Those on the south and at the east end are square-headed and labelled, of two-lights (one of three), and one has been badly altered. There is a small window at the west of the nave, now mutilated and closed, and placed to the north

Patricio Church : South Door of Chancel, as seen from the Inside.

of the western chapel, which is not equal to the nave in width, but only occupies the southern portion. The roof is open, coved, and ribbed with bosses. The chancel arch is Pointed, on octagonal columns. The chancel has an ugly modern ceiling encroaching on the arch. The great ecclesiological curiosities are the rood-loft, with its appendages, and the two stone altars which stand on its west side in the angles, besides the original altar in the western chapel. The rood-loft and screen are fairly complete, though, from neglect, out of repair. The screen has had some of its tracery broken. The loft has some very good open tracery and fine bands of foliage, and a course of Tudor flowers. The two altars placed against it are plain, wholly of stone, and some marks of the original crosses may be discerned on the slabs. In the north wall is a small projection, containing the steps which lead to the loft, and are pretty perfect. They are approached through a Pointed doorway, and lighted by small slits. There is a small window of three lights, with square head and label, giving light to the rood-loft on the south. Against the east wall of the chancel are two stone corbels, set low. The font has a circular bowl, on a low stem. The western chapel is about coeval with the church, and is entered on the south by a plain Pointed doorway. It has a solid wall to the east, against which is a third original stone altar, to the north of which, in the wall, is a Pointed trefoiled niche and two stone steps. On the south is a single-light window, trefoiled, and on the west side an obtuse-headed small window, closed. The interior is dark and dingy, with broken decayed pews, and is much neglected. The south porch contains a stoup. On the south side of the chancel, externally, is the plain stone ledge, seen also in Vowchurch and other churches of the neighbourhood. There is a curious old poor-box of wood. The interior flagged and poorly fitted up, and very dark. There is the shaft of a cross in the churchyard, which has a lych-gate. The situation is striking: on an eminence so steep that the latter part of the ascent is more like a staircase, and inaccessible to carriages. The view is lovely, over the neighbouring beautiful valley and woody hills.[1]

[1] For this church, see further, *Arch. Camb.*, 3rd Ser., vol. xi, p. 289; 3rd Ser., vol. iv, p. 145; 4th Ser., vol. v, p. 8; and for the inscribed font, 3rd Ser., vol. xi, p. 286. Also paper by F. R. Kempson in the *Transactions of the Woolhope Club*, 1883-5, p. 280. Very good photographs of the church, rood-screen, etc., can be obtained from Mr. J. Thirwall, 18, King Street, Hereford.

Penhow (St. John).

This church is small, but curious; the exterior whitewashed. It consists of a nave with south aisle, a tower in the centre of the south side and porch attached to it, and a chancel. The porch is large and plain. The western portion of the south aisle is divided by walling from the nave, the arches Pointed and plain, with octagonal pier, having square capital. There is a small Pointed arch between the tower and the aisle. Eastward of the tower, the aisle opens to the nave by two rather small Pointed arches without mouldings, upon a circular column which has a square abacus, and a capital enriched with curious foliage, intermixed with sculpture. The tower is low, and has a Pointed roof, tiled. On the north side of the nave are square-headed Perpendicular windows, Late and poor. At the west end of the nave is a lancet window, and at the west end of the south aisle another with trefoil head. The east window of the south aisle is Perpendicular and square-headed. At the east end of this aisle is a stone seat. The chancel is divided from the nave by a wall, whether ancient or more recent is not quite certain, but it appears to be original. In this is pierced a small arch, more of the proportions of a doorway, and on each side of it two square apertures, which have mouldings. The chancel is small and dark, has a double lancet at the east end, a single one on the north, and on the south a two-light window with tracery of doubtful character, whether Decorated or Perpendicular, probably the latter. In the north wall of the chancel is an ogee arch, feathered, with finial, under which was probably a tomb. The font has a circular bowl upon a small cylindrical shaft, on a square base. In the churchyard are a fine yew tree, and the base of a cross. The ruins of the adjacent castle are highly picturesque, but ugly farm-buildings are erected in the midst of them, and parts of the ancient walls applied to the same purpose. They are finely mantled in ivy. The prevailing character seems Late, but there is not much in a perfect state—the windows square-headed, and one large square tower has good bold machicolation.

Peterstone (St. Peter).

July 12, 1858.

A fine church, but in a desolate situation, and in a sadly dilapidated state, being too large for the scanty population. The whole is Perpendicular, and has considerable affinity to those of Somersetshire, across the Channel. The plan comprises a nave with north and south aisles, chancel, west tower, and south porch. The south aisle is not carried quite to the west of the nave. The south porch is extremely large, and has, like the south aisle, a moulded parapet with gurgoyles. There is a plain niche on the south porch. The doorway is continuous, and there are stone seats. The windows are of three lights, but some are mutilated, and only one remains unclosed on the north. On one of the south piers is a canopied ogee niche. There is a clerestory but without windows, and a mark appears on the east side of the tower, which shows that the roof must have been lowered. The arcades are quite of the Somersetshire sort, there are on each side four good moulded arches, with piers of closely-clustered shafts, having general capitals of rich foliage, but much clogged by whitewash. There is one arch on the north, narrower than the others, and the south arcade is frightfully out of the perpendicular. Over the piers are corbels, the roof very poor. The tower arch is Pointed, upon corbels. The chancel arch is continuous. There is a rood-door, and stairs on the north side of the chancel arch. In the south aisle a square-headed piscina, trefoiled, under a window, and one at the east end of the north aisle. There is a small space in the north aisle, partitioned off as a vestry. The chancel has been rebuilt in a very poor style. There are a few ancient open seats. The font has a plain octagonal bowl and panelled stem. The interior has a most desolate and dilapidated appearance. The tower is a fine one, having a richly-panelled battlement, the central piece on each side extended into a canopied niche, with pinnacles, and containing statues. At the north-east a lofty turret of octagonal form rises higher than the parapet, panelled with pinnacles. The belfry windows are each of two lights, that on the north having the pierced stonework so peculiar to the West; the buttresses are enriched with crocketed pinnacles attached. The tower is of three stages. The west window, of three lights, has in the jamb-moulding a delicate band of foliage with the branch. The large churchyard is shaded with fine trees, but contains no graves. There are six bells.

Rhymney (St. Augustine).

This is a large church, in the rude style prevalent in South Wales, consisting of a plain west tower, a nave of considerable length without aisles, a chancel, and south porch. The porch, as is usual in this part of the country, is very large, resembling a transept, and is entered by a Pointed arch, moulded, near which is a benatura, somewhat mutilated. The tower is small in proportion to the length of the church, has no buttresses or stringcourse of division, but plain battlements, and four small crocketed pinnacles. On the west side is a doorway, with moulded semicircular arch and elegant clustered shafts of Early English character. The belfry windows are plain Perpendicular, of two lights; the other openings of the tower very narrow and square-headed. The nave has a tiled roof, that of the chancel slated. The church being more spacious than required by the parish, the western portion of the nave is divided off by a screen and not used. The interior has the usual naked and desolate appearance, though not out of repair. The tower opens to the nave by a low

Pointed arch, resembling a door. The roof has plain ribs, forming a semicircular arch. The windows are few and mostly square-headed, late Perpendicular, of three lights; in some are fragments of painted glass. At the east end of the nave, near the chancel arch, are two small windows, set low in the wall, on opposite sides, and on the south side another set above, which must have been intended to light the rood-loft. The chancel arch is Pointed, with continuous mouldings. On the south side, at some elevation, is the door opening to the rood-loft, together with the steps. On the north side of the chancel arch is a bracket, having some of the rope and knotted ornament, apparently Early, but clogged with whitewash. The chancel is large but gloomy. The east and the north windows being closed up, those on the south are Late Perpendicular and brought down low, but there is no indication of sedilia. The chancel roof is different from that of the nave, but plain and open, the rafters crossing. The font is a plain octagonal bowl. The church is paved with large stones for flagging. There are five bells.

Rockfield (St. Kenelm).

September 27, 1847.

A small church, in a pretty situation, consisting only of a chancel and nave, south porch, and small western tower. The latter is finely mantled in ivy, and has some plain square-headed slits. It is crowned by a wooden turret, with tiled roof. The east window is of three lights, and Third Pointed; other windows of the chancel are single and square-headed, narrow and plain; those of the nave are square-headed, of three lights, and of Third Pointed character. The chancel arch is pointed, without shafts. Over the east gable is a cross, and the roofs are flagged externally. The pews are high. In the churchyard is a fine cross, lately well restored.

St. Arvan's.

June 4, 1849.

A very poor church, greatly modernised. It consists of chancel, nave, and a modern west tower of octagonal form. The external walls are whitewashed, and most of the windows modern insertions. There is the trace of an Early Norman doorway, now closed, on the south side of the chancel; the arch is very narrow and has imposts, one of which is plain, the other ornamented with carving. The church has no north windows. The east window is Late and debased; on the south one of two lancets, under a Pointed arch. The chancel arch is a modern one. On the north side of the nave are some large solid buttresses, resembling sheds, which may be original.

St. Bride (Netherwent).

July 13, 1858.

Like Marshfield and Peterstone, this church is situated on the extensive level, or marsh, which reaches to the Bristol Channel. It consists of a nave with short north aisle or chapel (now closed), chancel, west tower, and south porch. The whole appears Perpendicular, but, except the tower, does not much partake of the fine Somersetshire character apparent at Peterstone. The tower is, however, a fine and remarkable one, of good stone, divided by two horizontal strings, and having an octagonal turret at the north-east. The tower resembles, in many respects, that of Peterstone, but on its north and west sides the parapet seems to be left unfinished, having no battlement nor panelling, but rising into a pediment in the centre, both on the west and on the east. On these two sides the parapet has fine panelling, and there is a fine canopied niche occupying the central battlement on the south. There are corner buttresses and pinnacles, which last are small. The turret rises above the tower parapet, and is surmounted by fine panelling. The west window is of three lights, and below it is a doorway. The porch is, as usual, very large. Its inner doorway is of Tudor form, with label upon corbel heads; its mouldings flowered. A canopied niche over the outer door has crockets, finial, and groining. The outer doorway is plain. The interior is tolerably neat, but rather desolate, and the long nave has been divided by a modern partition, the eastern part of it alone being sufficient for the small congregation. The roof is coved, with ribs on corbels, and bosses at the points of intersection. The north chapel, which is closed, is separated from the nave by two good Perpendicular arches, rising from a pier of clustered shafts, having flowered general capital, and a canopied ogee niche on one of the hollows between the shafts. The windows are of three lights, and have Perpendicular tracery. Near the pulpit, in the south wall, is a stone bracket. The tower arch is lofty and continuous. The northern windows are closed. In the south wall of the nave is a very small flat ogee recess. The chancel arch is good Perpendicular, of Somersetshire character, with small shafts and continuous mouldings. The east window is is of three lights. On the south side of the chancel is one square-headed, of two lights, and one single. On the south of the altar is an old-looking shallow recess, in the corner of which is a small trough, like a piscina. The font is small octagonal, on a stem raised on two steps. There is a part of a cross on the south side. The churchyard has no graves. No burials seem to take place either at St. Bride's or Peterstone, perhaps because of the moisture of the churchyards. The parishioners probably bury at Coedkernew and at Marshfield.

St. Mellons.

September 10, 1843.

This church has nave, chancel, tower, and porch on the south side, a south aisle continued from the tower to the east end of the chancel, and a north chapel to the latter. This arrangement is rather complicated. The exterior entirely whitewashed. The porch is very large, its roof covered, and within it a benatura. The tower something like that of Rhymney, without buttresses and rude in workmanship; the parapet embattled, belfry windows square-headed, and other openings small and rude. The windows are all Perpendicular, of three lights, with good tracery; some parts of the church may be earlier, but the character is rude and coarse. The interior is gloomy, and has a neglected appearance; the pews are painted white, but only occupy a portion of the church. The roofs of the body and aisle are separate and tiled. The arch from the nave to the chancel is wide and straight-sided; the chancel is not equal to the nave in breadth; the arches dividing the aisle ranging with the pier of the chancel arch, and a small arch opening to the aisle on the north side of the chancel arch. The pier between these two is octagonal. There is a moulded arch of plain character between the chancel and aisle. The south aisle, beyond the tower, opens to the nave by two Pointed arches, springing from circular columns, and between the south aisle and the chancel is an arch with continuous mouldings and no shafts. The roof of the nave has ribs forming panels, and a wood cornice. There are two square recesses in the south wall of the nave, near the west end. There was evidently an altar at the east end of the south aisle, which is a little elevated. In the wall is an elegant niche, the pedestal of which is enriched with foliage. One of the south windows has the sill extended with a small octagonal piscina. Over the east end of the south aisle is a boarded panelled roof. On the north side of the chancel are the steps that led to the rood-loft. There are several stone brackets in the chancel. The font has rather a small moulded octagonal bowl, upon a panelled pedestal of Perpendicular character. The interior is much clogged with ugly paint. The graves are adorned with flowers. There are five bells.

St. Woollos (Newport).

An interesting church, principally Norman, consisting of a nave and chancel with side aisles, a small north transept, south porch, a curious chapel to the west of the nave, forming now a vestibule, and a tower westward of it. The tower, porch, and almost all the windows are Perpendicular, but the main part of the nave is Norman. The tower is rather plain, having a battlement and octagonal turret at the north-east, the belfry window square-headed, and on the west side a canopied niche. The south porch is disused as an entrance, and applied as a vestry. The windows of the north aisle and transepts are of four lights, some others are of three lights, and some square-headed. The roofs are tiled. The western chapel, called that of St. Mary, is Early English of rather plain character, consequently later than the Norman nave. It has externally a corbel table beneath the roof, and on each side three lancet windows; and within it are four arches in the wall for tombs, two of which on the south contain mutilated effigies: one of a knight apparently of the fifteenth century; one earlier is cross-legged, with rich chain armour and shield. On the north side, under one of the arches, is an alabaster effigy of a female, with a necklace, but the head has disappeared. The tower arch opening to the chapel is Pointed, and wide with continuous mouldings. The west gable of the nave is crowned by a cross; between the lady chapel and the nave is a very grand Norman doorway, which was originally the entrance to the church, though the chapel was added at no very distant period from the erection of the nave. This arch has four courses of moulding, containing chevron and billeted ornaments, rising from shafts which have curiously-sculptured capitals, with acanthus foliage and figures of animals. The nave is divided from each aisle by five semicircular arches, springing from large cylindrical columns, with the common inverted capitals and square abaci. Over each column a clerestory window, with semicircular arch of like character with the main arches, and now opening into the aisles, the roofs of which have been raised at a subsequent period. Beyond the Norman arches, on the north side, is a small narrow addition or

St. Woollos Church : Norman Doorway.

chapel, which opens by a moulded Pointed arch; and opposite to it (on the south) is a window in the wall. The transept contains nothing particular, but there is a small arch obliquely set between the north aisle and the small added chapel. Near this is a small turret with stairs that led to the rood-loft, and on the south side a small square-headed Perpendicular window, which must have given light to it. The chancel is in two divisions, the eastern forming a kind of sanctuary. The chancel arch is hidden by a gallery. On the south side of the chancel is a Decorated window, of two lights. The east window is hidden by a huge modern reredos of Italian woodwork, in which a picture is inserted. On the south side of the altar is a large tomb of the debased Italian style, but mutilated. On the north side a plain arch in the wall, within which is a mutilated effigy of a female under a trefoil canopy. Under one of the monuments in the chancel is a real skull. The nave is much impaired in appearance by large galleries which encroach sadly upon the arches. In the western one is a large organ. The font has a square bowl. The situation of the church is elevated and striking, commanding a very grand and varied view.

Skenfrith (St. Bridget).

September 27, 1847.

The church comprises a nave and aisles, a chancel with south chapel, western steeple, and south porch. The architectural features are mixed, and there are good specimens of the three Pointed styles, with some of the local peculiarities of the district. The aisles are wide, and the roofs of nave and aisles are separate and coved, having internally ribbed panelling. The arcade on each side of the nave is First Pointed. There are four bays, with Pointed arches, springing from low circular columns with moulded capitals; those on the north have square, those on the south circular, bases. At the west end of the north aisle is a very good Middle Pointed window of four lights, of the Herefordshire type. The north aisle has tie-beams; the east gable of the north aisle is very acute, and of good masonry. In the north aisle are some windows, also of a Herefordshire kind, of three lights, without tracery or foils, and apparently transitional from First to Middle Pointed. The chancel arch is First Pointed, springing from octagonal shafts; that on the south has a toothed capital, but much clogged with whitewash. In the angle north of this arch is a First Pointed bracket. The south aisle has Third Pointed windows; that at the west of four lights. The tower arch is low, and of contracted form, with imposts. The chancel has an east window, like that described in the north aisle, containing some good pieces of stained glass. The north-east window of the chancel is Middle Pointed, of two lights; the south-east window is Third Pointed, of three lights, and below it is a semicircular piscina with mouldings. The chancel has a narrow chapel in the south side, opening to it by a Tudor arch on octagonal shafts; there is another arch, with continuous mouldings, between this chapel and the south aisle of the nave. This chapel has Late Third Pointed windows. The tower is First Pointed, and has thick walls, with lancets on the north and south sides; also a string-course and west door, with tolerable mouldings. The tower is low, and surmounted by a wooden belfry, tiled, and resembling a dovecot. The font is an octagonal bowl on a circular stem, with square base chamfered at the angles. There is a Jacobean pulpit, and much pewing of the same age, and some open benches. There is a tomb to some members of the family of Morgan, with incised figures of a man and woman, A.D. 1587. Over the south door is a niche. The porch has open square-headed windows, and in the angle a stoup, with mutilated trefoil-headed fenestella. The material is a reddish stone.

In bringing to a close these "Notes on the Older Welsh Churches," it will be well to record briefly their story. The writer, Sir Stephen Richard Glynne, Baronet, of Hawarden Castle, the first President of the Cambrian Archæological Association, was an indefatigable archæologist and especially devoted to ecclesiology. Probably no man in the kingdom ever visited so many of the old churches of the land; certainly no one ever examined so large a number so thoroughly and intelligently, or recorded so minutely their details and salient features. It was his custom on these visits to note down very carefully all the points of interest, and afterwards to write them out more fully in a series of MS. note-books. From those relating to England there have been published already his *Notes on the Churches of Kent*.

Those Note-books, which contained the churches in Wales, were kindly placed by his nephew, the late Mr. William H. Gladstone, at my service for the pages of the *Archæologia Cambrensis*, in whose volumes instalments have appeared for many years, and they are now completed.

At first it was decided to add footnotes to the descriptions, so as to bring them down to date: and for those relating to the diocese of St. Asaph I am myself responsible; and I have to record my obligations to the late Dean Allen for those in the earlier portion of St. David's. After the Dean's death, it was thought best to omit the footnotes, and to print only the notes themselves; for their value depended not on the subsequent additions, but on their own intrinsic merit as full and accurate descriptions of the churches at the time indicated. The "Notes" in the MS. books follow no particular order of time or place, but were entered according to the opportunities of visiting the churches. In transcribing them for the press, they were at first put together in alphabetical order, according to their diocese and deanery. Subsequently, however, this plan had to be abandoned; but in the later dioceses of Bangor and Llandaff they have been arranged alphabetically in their counties. Any inconvenience arising from this change, however, will be obviated by the Index. As the "Notes" cover the period ranging from 1824 to 1874, they will be seen to include a vast number of churches which have been greatly altered by renovation, and some altogether rebuilt. This adds greatly to their value as a record, not only of the then state of the churches, but of much that has now ceased to exist. Besides which, the interest in local, and not least in parochial, history, has been greatly developed in the last few years, and these "Notes" will supply useful and reliable information on the ground they cover. Above all, it must not be forgotten how much the fabrics of our parish churches have to tell us of the periods when, as well as of the methods by which, revived church life expressed itself in the past. Indeed, our older parish churches are visible object-lessons, that tell us by monument and effigy and epitaph of our forbears, and illustrate, by capital and moulding, by arch and window, when the forefathers of the parish bestirred themselves, in successive generations, to beautify their House of Prayer. Whether the detail belong to the "Norman," or one of the three "Pointed" styles—for this is the title by which Sir Stephen marks the Early English, the Decorated, and the Perpendicular—or whether it be of still later date, it hands down to us a visible and legible illustration of the real continuity, under differing external conditions, of the old Mother Church of the land.

February 25th, 1902.

D. R. Thomas.

EFFIGY OF SIR S. R. GLYNNE, BART., IN HAWARDEN CHURCH.